WILD LIFE

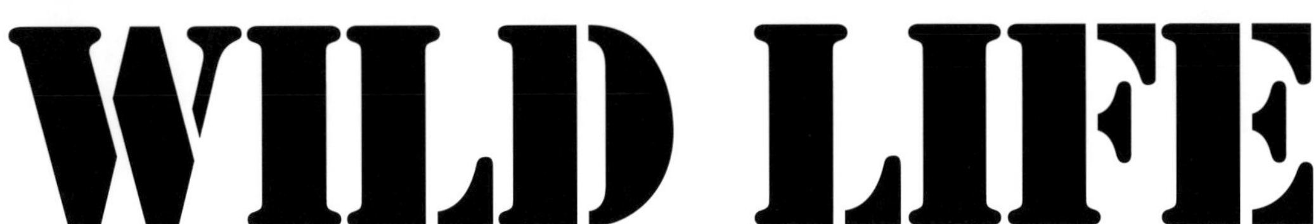
WILD LIFE

ELIZABETH MURRAY

JESSI REAVES

CONTEMPORARY ARTS MUSEUM HOUSTON
DANCING FOXES PRESS, BROOKLYN, NEW YORK

CONTENTS

6

15

INSERT

42

74

75

76

78

RUDE AWAKENING:
1940/1986
REBECCA MATALON

PLATES

PROFILE:
ELIZABETH MURRAY
KATE HORSFIELD
(1986)

A CONVERSATION:
JOHANNA FATEMAN
JESSI REAVES
(2019)

DIRECTOR'S AFTERWORD
CURATOR'S ACKNOWLEDGMENTS

EXHIBITION VIEWS

BIOGRAPHIES

RUDE AWAKENING: 1940/1986

Rebecca Matalon

Forty-six years separate the births of Elizabeth Murray and Jessi Reaves. The two artists did not know each other, nor would their time as makers overlap. When Murray passed away in 2007, she had been painting and drawing for more than four decades. Reaves did not begin exhibiting her own sculptural assemblages—which most often take the form of functional furniture—for another seven years, and while she has consistently done so since, she is in many ways just beginning to build an equally idiosyncratic and familiar body of work.

The generations dividing the artists are significant. Born in 1940, Murray came of age during the civil rights movement and second-wave feminism, bearing witness to the radical politics of the 1960s and 1970s and later to the conservative backlash of the 1980s and 1990s. Reaves, a child of the 1980s, grew up amid the economic boom of the following decade and emerged from college in 2009 amid a collapsing US economy. The different historical, political, and cultural contexts, as well as the varying mediums, of the two artists' works might make their pairing curious if not quickly apparent. Yet there are intriguing formal and thematic affinities that encourage such a juxtaposition: Both artists employ muddy palettes, ungainly shapes, and uneven surface textures. Both are just as likely to mix up those qualities with bright colors, cartoonish forms, and "feminine" motifs, such as bows and patchwork. Both artists mine imagery of the body and of domestic places, only to render these broken, unruly, chaotic, wild, and sensuous sites.

Beyond formal and thematic parallels, the two bodies of works are bound by indeterminacy; the associations held in their forms and images are manifold, at times ambiguous and even contradictory. These internal conflicts extend to the experience of viewing their works, which tend to simultaneously evoke pleasure and repulsion. Reaves's lush and supple surfaces beckon. And I confess a desire to reach out and caress Murray's paintings to learn of their textures. Likewise, both artists' allusions to bodily forms and fluids are dizzying if not disturbing. In their works, Reaves and Murray present the body and the home as containers for the tensions between internal and external realities and appearances. *Wild Life: Elizabeth Murray & Jessi Reaves* examines the myriad implications of depicting the body and the home as continuously coming together and falling apart and asks what distinguishes, in this regard, Reaves in our contemporary moment from Murray in the 1970s, 1980s, and 1990s.

Over the past six years, Jessi Reaves has produced a prodigious body of work that is situated at the intersection of sculpture and home-furniture design. Her works variously take the forms of chairs, couches, ottomans, tables, lamps, and shelves and are made of a mix of found and fabricated elements.

After graduating from the Rhode Island School of Design in 2009, Reaves moved to New York and took on various odd jobs—sewing curtains, upholstering pillows, and, eventually, working in a furniture-design studio centered on midcentury-modern reproductions. Given free rein to work on her own projects after hours using the shop's tools and discarded materials, Reaves began to make art after having spent several years without access to such resources. Reflecting on her emotional and psychic struggles in this period, she has noted the ways that the functionality of furniture provided an entry back into art making by allowing for failure and/or success in one form or another.[1] Granting her work a "functional potential . . . felt perverse"—she claims it was the "one thing I knew I really shouldn't do"—but was liberating.[2] Reaves's reflections are telling: they demarcate the hybridity and indeterminacy of her objects from the outset—part sculpture, part furniture. Such hybridity specifically disallows singularity and manifests a twofold rebuke: Her chairs can be sat in, tables worked at, and lamps used to illuminate, all embodying a functionality that transgresses fine art's purely symbolic value and resists Western art history's hierarchy of valuation that has for centuries placed the fine arts above the applied arts. Indeed, this will for transgression runs throughout the artist's work to date.

From the outset, Reaves's works, as outgrowths of the design studio where she once worked, have routinely incorporated modernist furniture—sometimes in fragments and sometimes whole—as their structural basis. Marcel Breuer's Cesca armchair (1928), Josef Hoffmann and Josef Frank's A811 armchair (1920s), Isamu Noguchi's Noguchi table (1947) and Akari lamp (1951), and Ludwig Mies van der Rohe and Lilly Reich's Barcelona chair (1929) are just a few of the iconic objects that made their way in. Modern furniture design, cohering around a midcentury paradigm of formalist reduction and rational order, eschewed imagery deemed nonessential or in any way decorative. Functionality, affordability, efficiency of forms and materials, and an emphasis on the machine-made were paramount to the modernists, who in a radical and decisive break with nineteenth-century ideas denounced ornate wallpaper, drapery, upholstery, and other embellishments, deeming them not only excessive and unnecessary but vulgar and even—according to architect Adolf Loos—"criminal."[3] By embellishing such objects, mass-produced with an economy of form following Mies's "less-is-more" tenet, Reaves defies a history in which ornament and craft are assumed irreconcilable.[4] She corrupts their purported purity through modifications that point to the ways that the decorative haunts modernist design by its very exclusion. As one of many twentieth-century movements defined by negation, modernism is inherently bound up with what it seeks to repress.

Reaves's works offer up objects that embrace modernism *and* decoration, sculpture *and* furniture, while recognizing yet another binary: that of the "masculine/feminine."[5] Her series of works featuring found modernist furniture wrapped in silk and nylon textiles call particular attention to the split between the male-dominated field of design and materials traditionally associated with women's garments. For *Maraschino Fairy* (2014) and *Slipcovered Chair (Pink Gag)* (2017), Reaves sheathes modernist design icons in gauzy pink fabrics. Layered over Hoffmann and Frank's caned and raw wood form in the case of *Maraschino Fairy* and, in the latter, Breuer's caning and tubular steel frame, the clingy fabrics resemble lingerie, as if, as the artist has suggested, the chairs have "slipped into something more comfortable."[6] The inclusion of a single zipper running along the chairbacks heightens the sense that they have dresses on, while also implying that they could just as easily animate to slip them back off. Reaves, who claims that these works "feminize" such objects, performs an erotic act of adornment, tarting up smooth, clean lines and aesthetic purity with color and material culturally coded as feminine only since the 1950s, at the apex of modernism. Arguably, in dressing them up, Reaves makes the original chairs seem almost immodest; she turns the tables on their modernism, suggesting that crudeness lies not in ornamentality but in bareness.

Maraschino Fairy and *Slipcovered Chair* are unique in their simplicity; Reaves's only modification to the modernist icons is the addition of the slipcovers. By contrast, her interventions are multiple in *Cesca Leaves the Stack (Modified Chair)* (2016) [p. 67]. Between Breuer's iconic chair and a translucent nylon sheath, the artist has affixed raw foam, cushioning the surfaces where body

1. See Jessi Reaves, interview by Johanna Fateman, in this volume, 44.
2. Ibid.
3. See Adolf Loos, *Ornament and Crime: Selected Essays* (Riverside, CA: Ariadne Press, 1998).
4. For a more extended consideration of Reaves's work's relationship to a history of modernist design, see Charlotte Ickes, "The Surface of Stuff: The Stuff of Surface," in *Ginny Casey and Jessi Reaves* (Philadelphia: Institute of Contemporary Art, University of Pennsylvania, 2018), 15–61.
5. Jessi Reaves, in "An Ideological Revision of Furniture Design: Josephine Graf in Conversation with Jessi Reaves," *Mousse*, no. 52 (February–March 2016): 232.
6. Ibid.

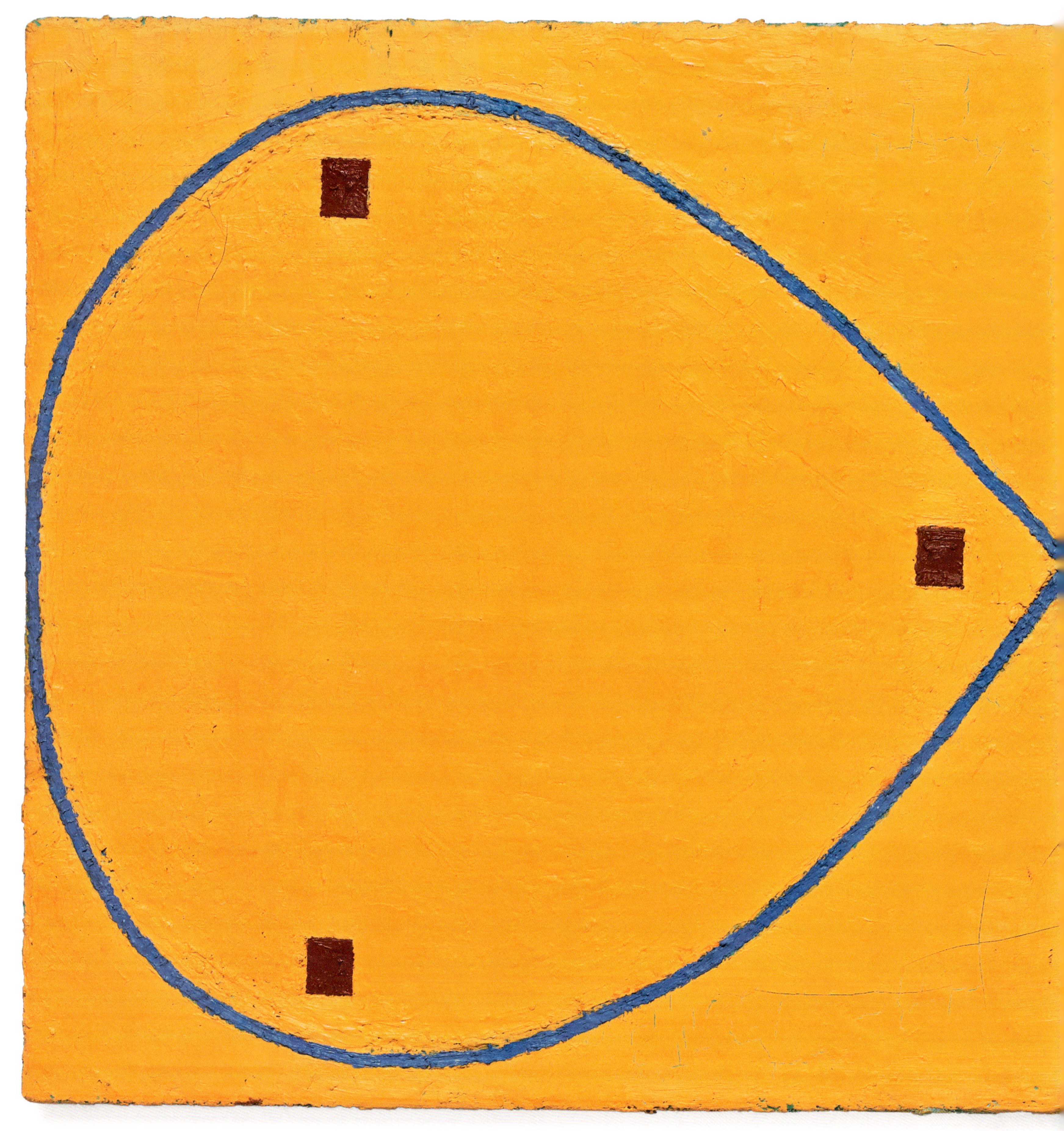

Elizabeth Murray, Mobius Band, 1974
Oil on canvas
14 × 28 inches (35.6 × 71.1 cm)

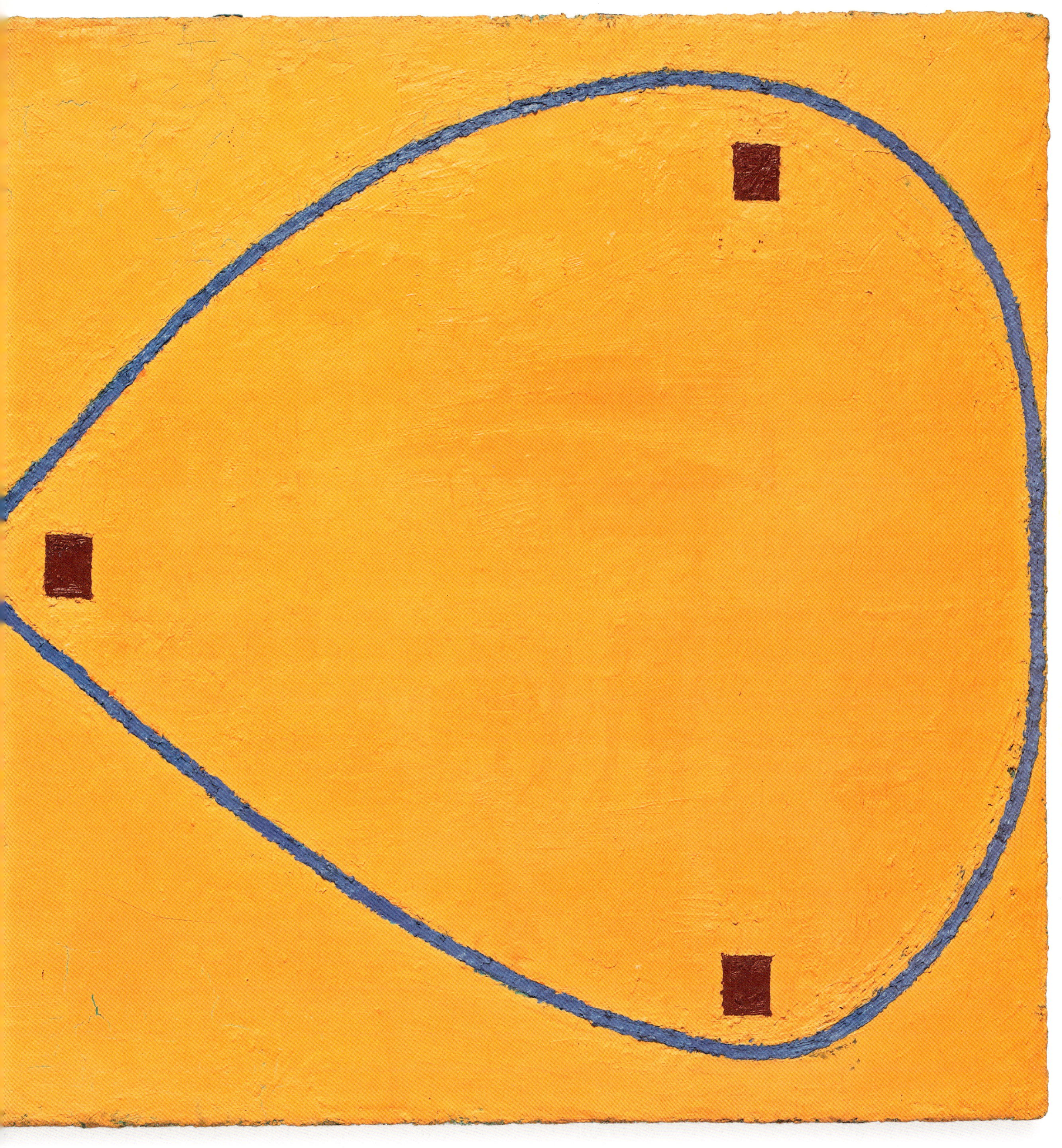

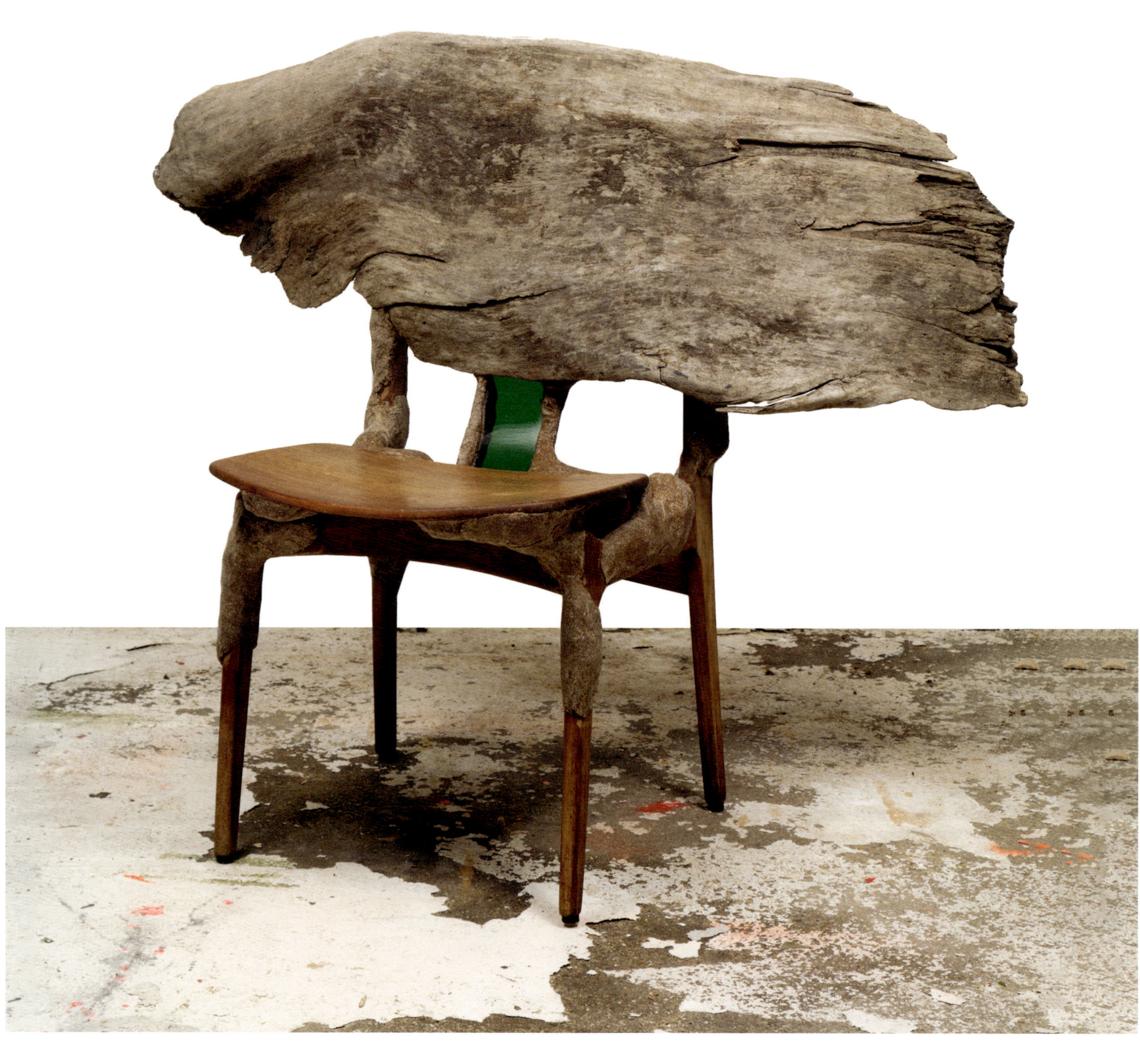

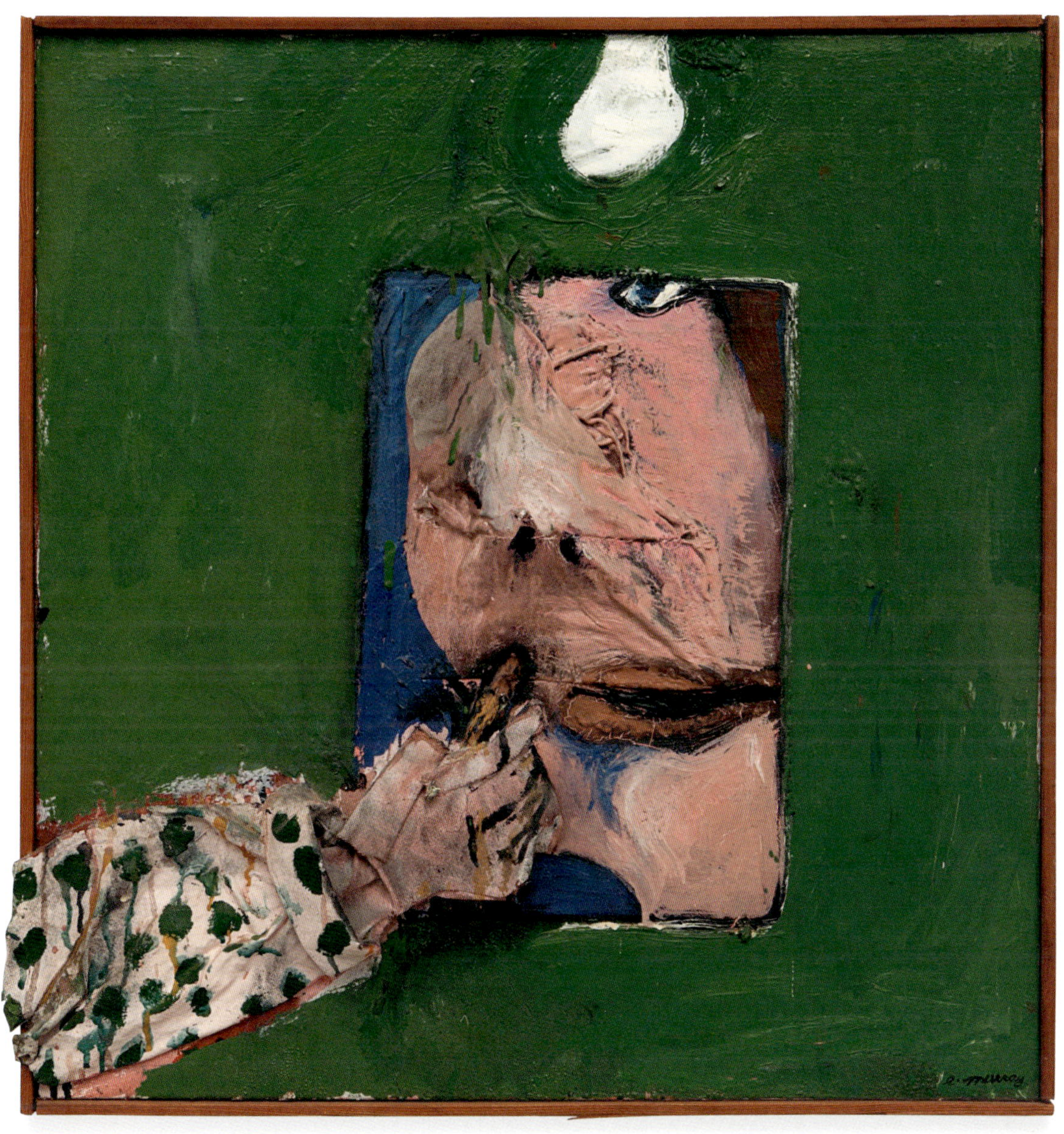

OPPOSITE
Jessi Reaves, Drift Wood Chair, 2016
Teak, driftwood, studio dust, wood glue, plexiglass, and hardware
38 × 47 × 29 inches (96.5 × 119.4 × 73.7 cm)

ABOVE
Elizabeth Murray, N. H. Lockwood, 1963–67
Oil and cloth on canvas in wood frame
26 1/4 × 25 3/8 inches (66.7 × 64.5 cm)

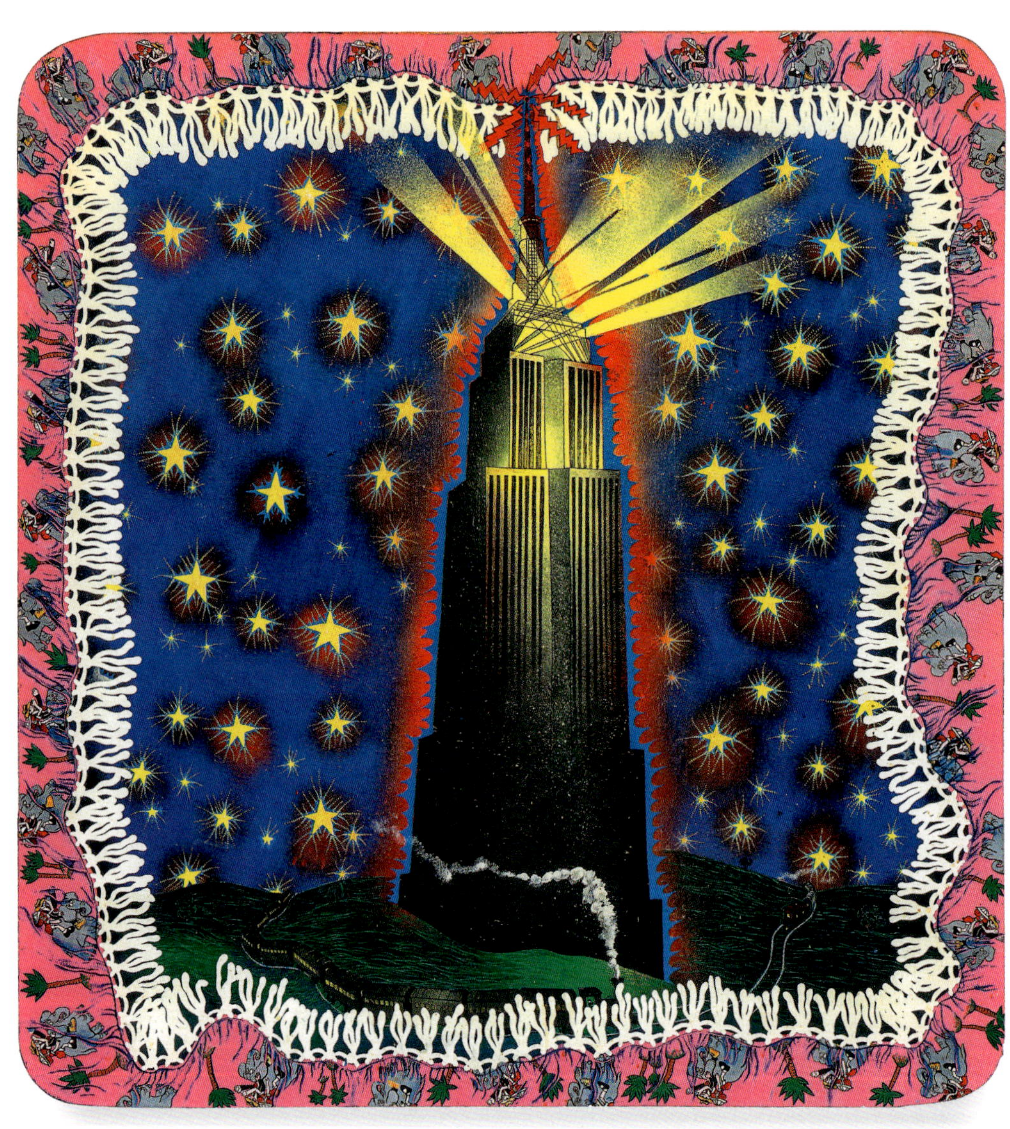

Elizabeth Murray, Night Empire, 1967–68
Oil on canvas
51 1/2 × 48 1/4 inches (130.8 × 123.2 cm)

OPPOSITE
Jessi Reaves, Engine Room Shelving (Recollection Wedding Edition), 2015
Pine, polyurethane foam, vinyl, and linen
70 × 50 × 21 inches (177.8 × 127 × 53.3 cm)

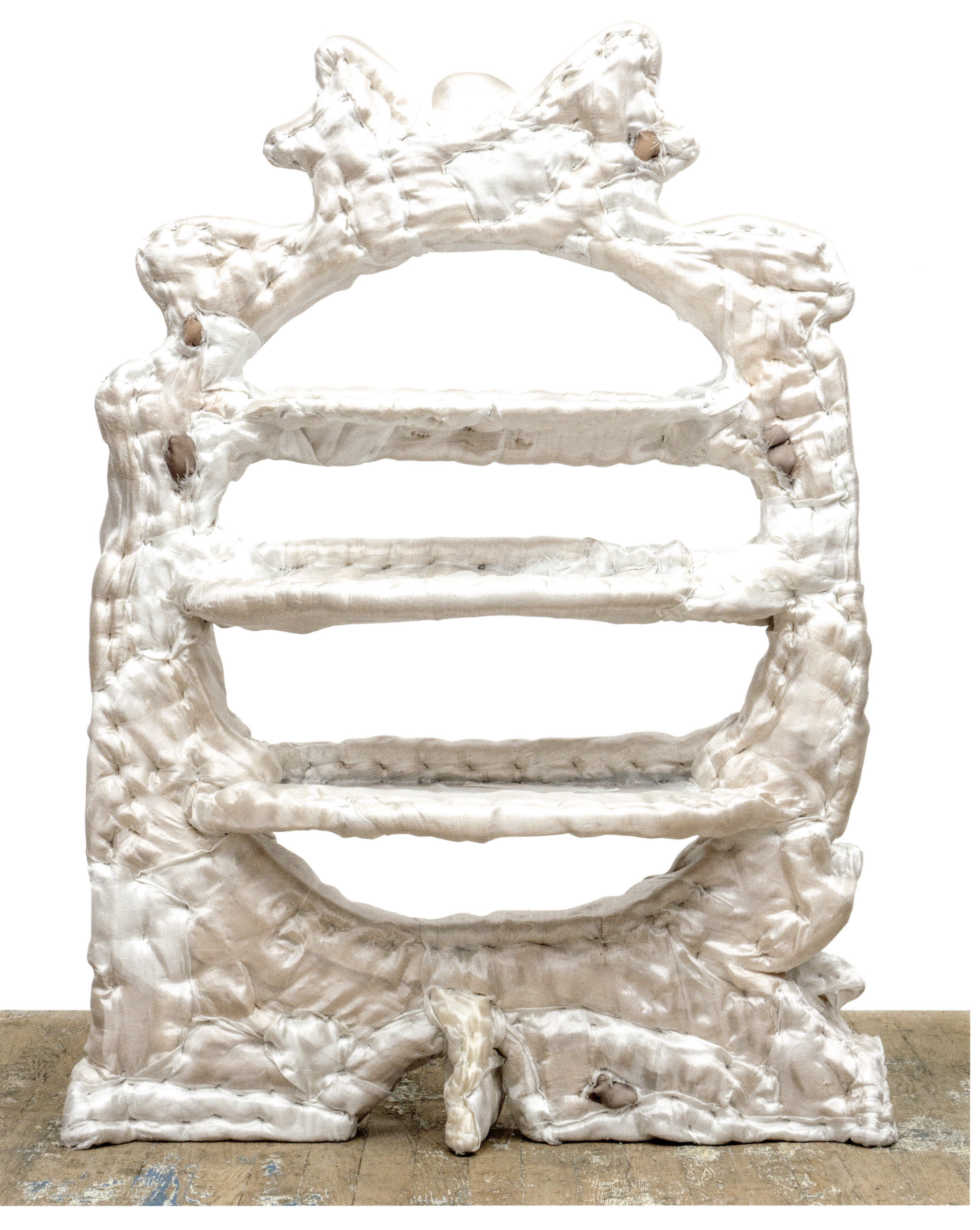

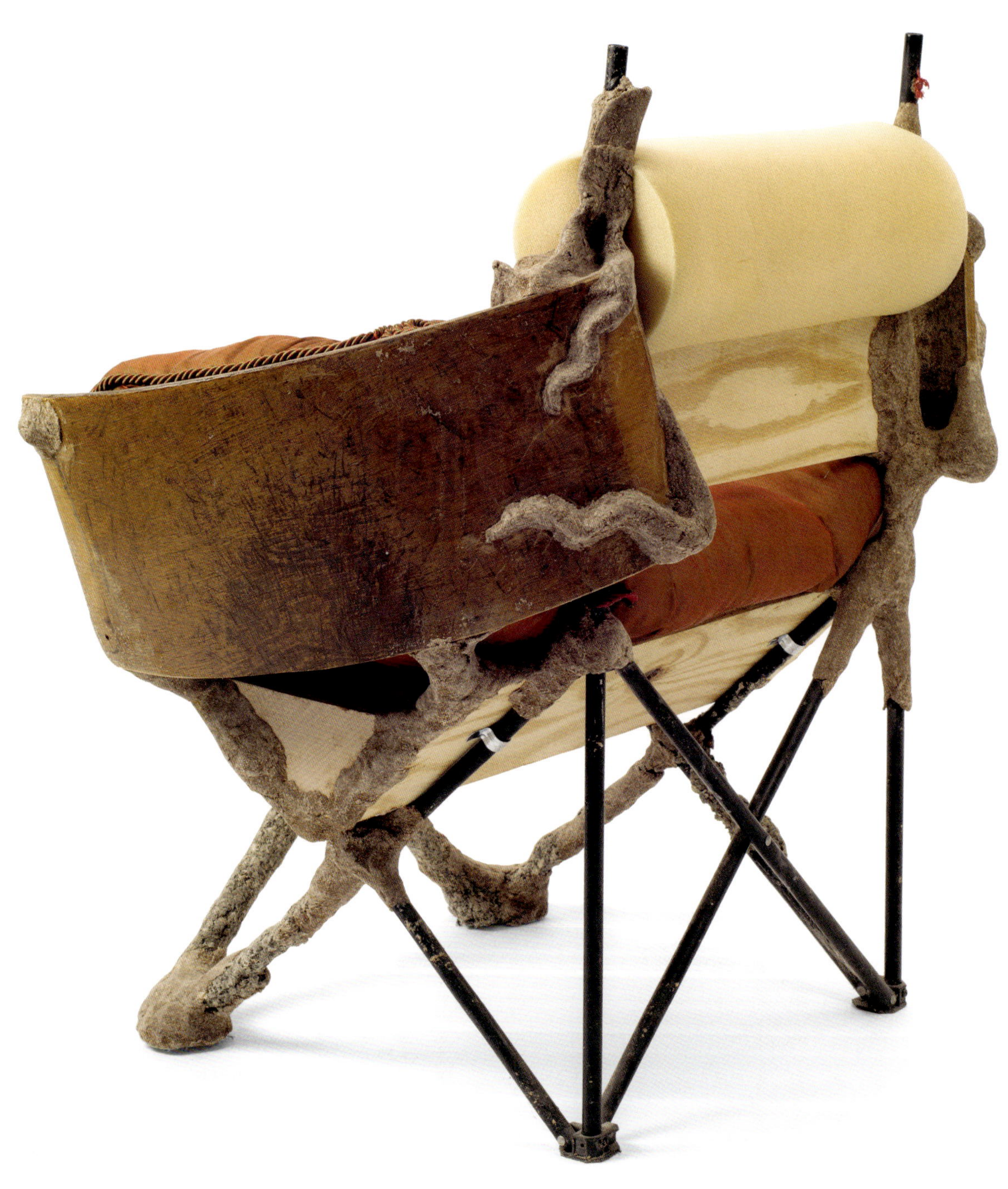

Jessi Reaves, Crust Bucket Comes to Town (Slipper Chair), 2016
Steel frame, pine, studio dust, wood glue, polyurethane foam, cotton, silk, plywood, nylon, cording, and hardware
36 × 38 × 38 inches (91.4 × 96.5 × 96.5 cm)

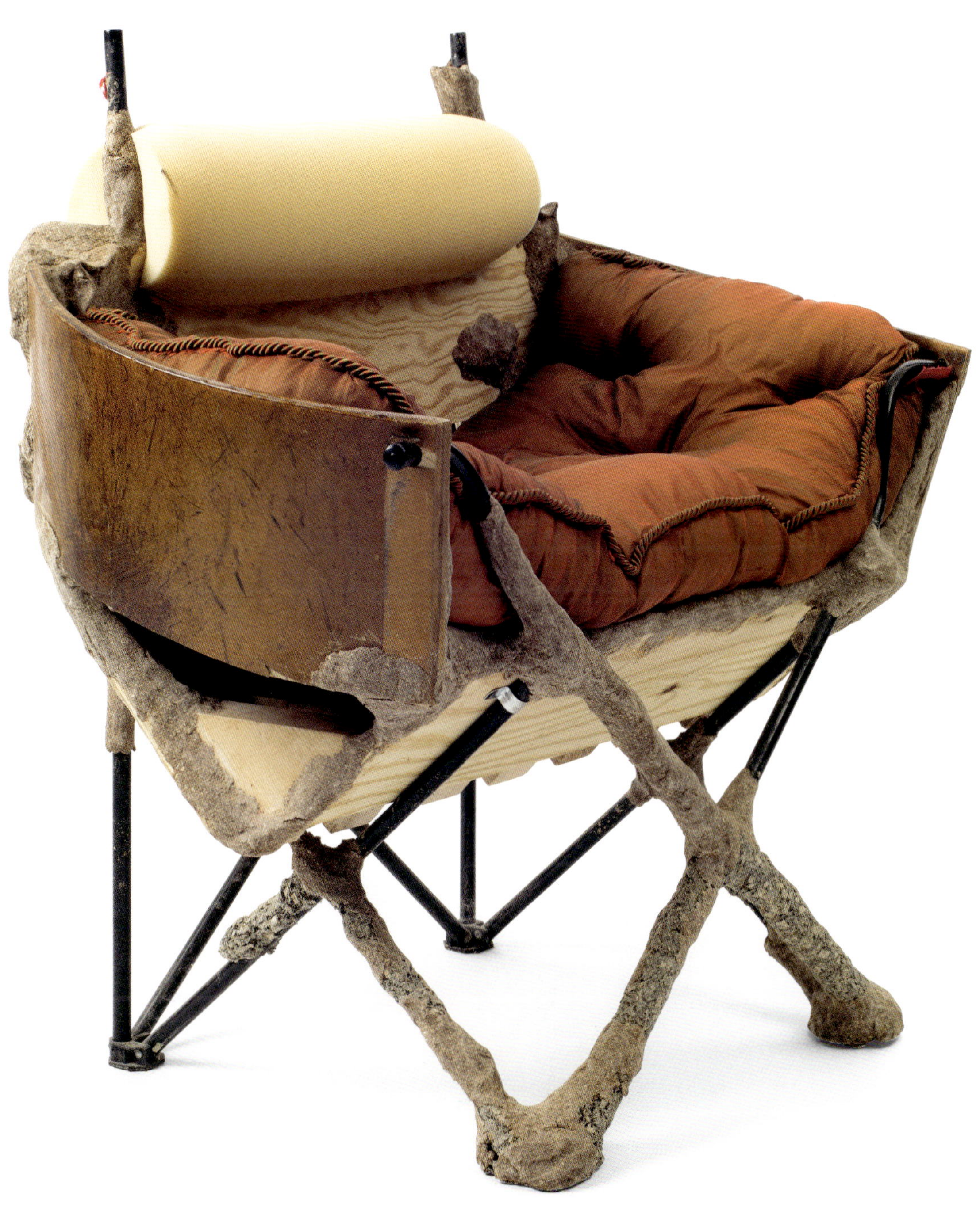

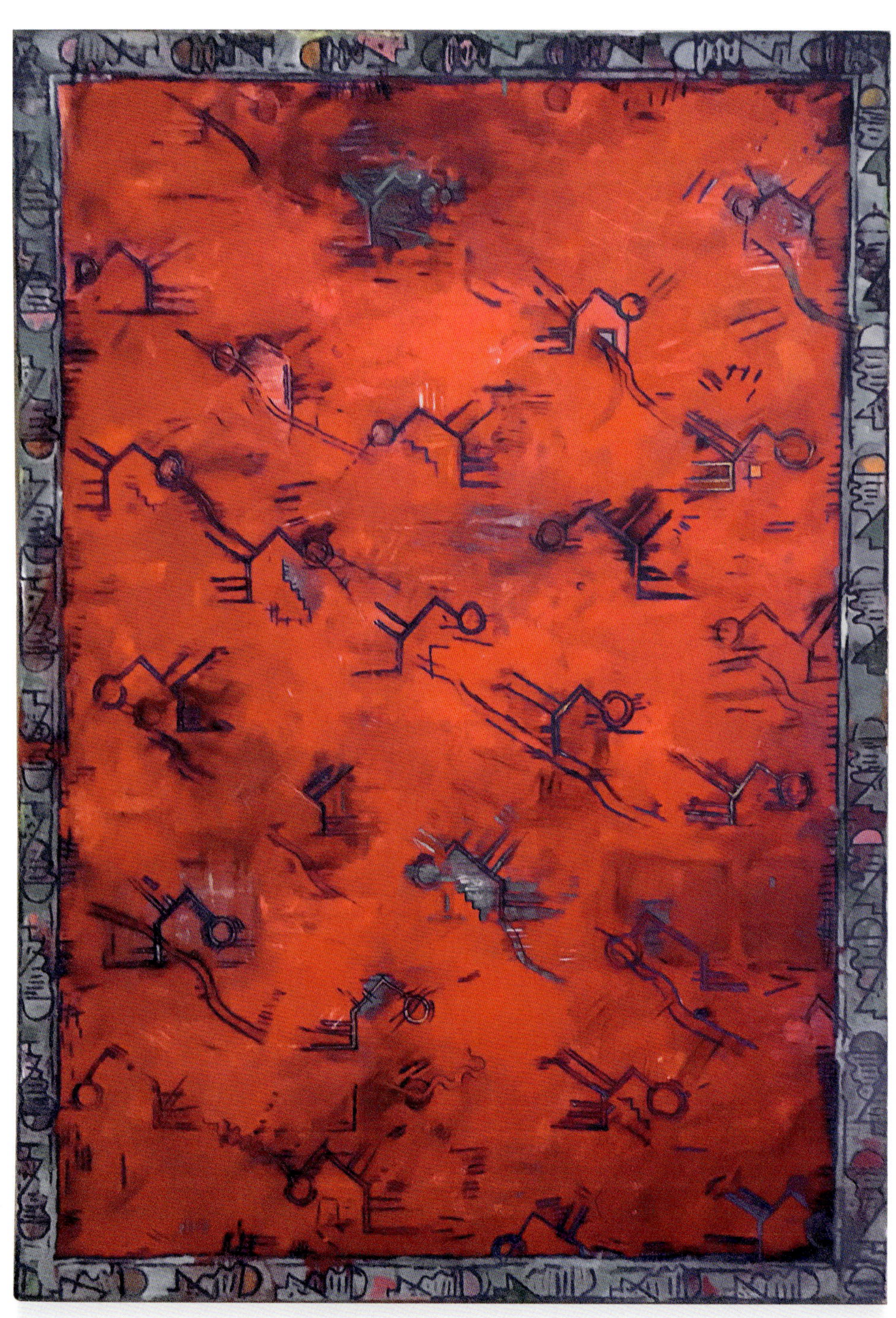

Elizabeth Murray, Dakota's Red, 1971
Oil on canvas
69 × 46 1/8 inches (175.3 × 117.2 cm)
24

P R O F I L E

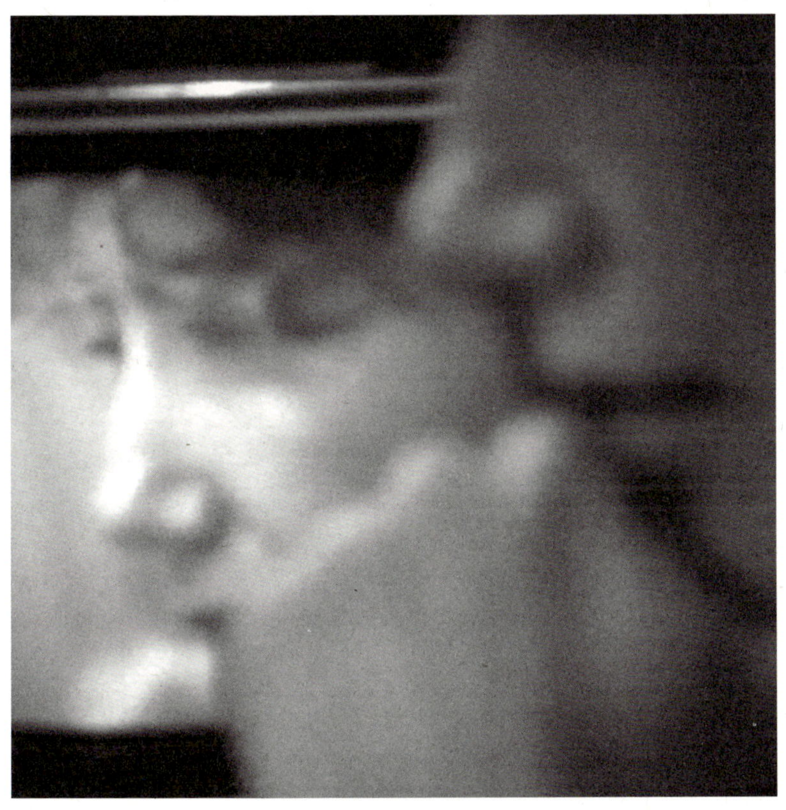

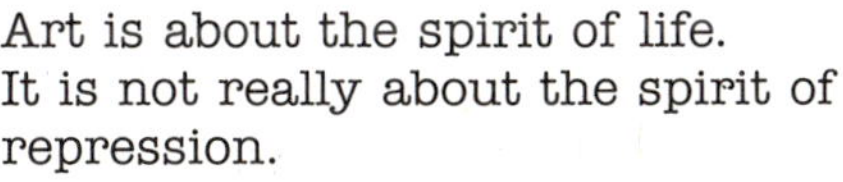

Art is about the spirit of life.
It is not really about the spirit of
repression.

ELIZABETH MURRAY

PROFILE VOL. 5
NO. 3 SUMMER 1986
$3.00

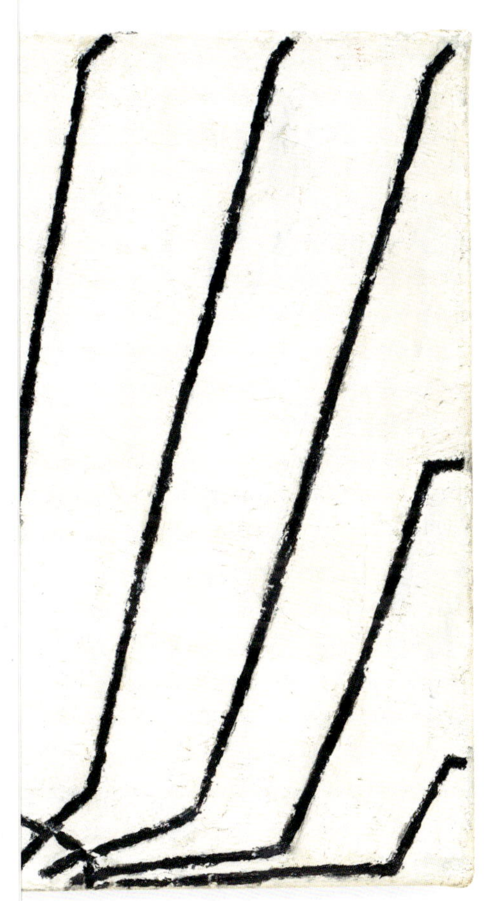

VIDEO DATA BANK

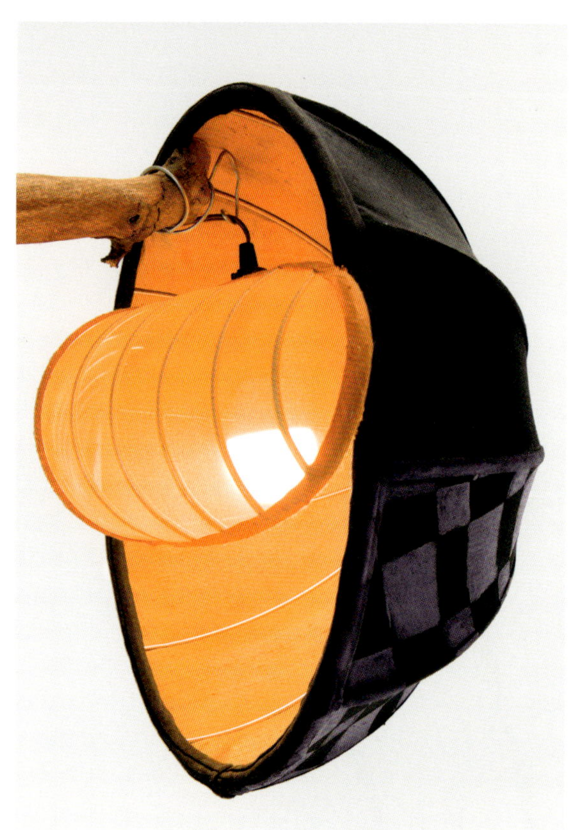

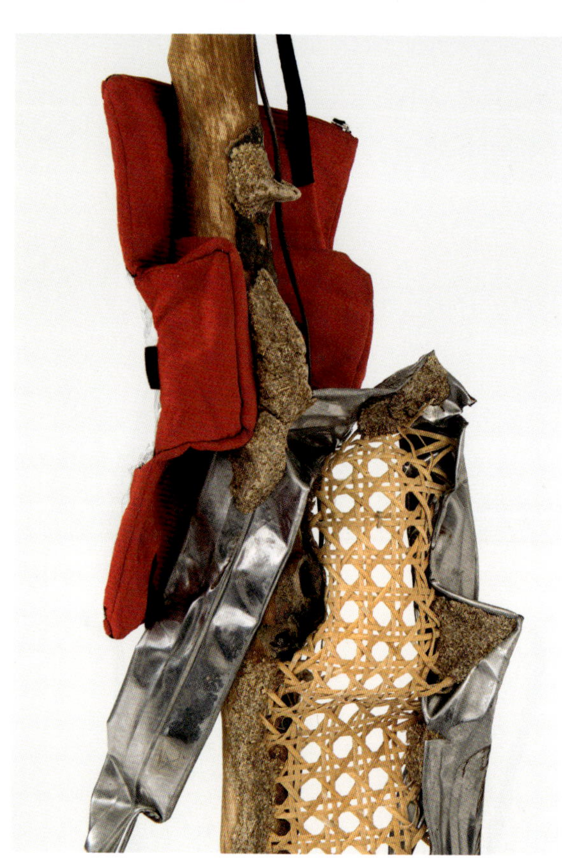

Jessi Reaves, Lamp for a Road House, 2017
NYC stick, metal, gaining, fabric, paint, plastic, and lamp wiring
96 × 62 × 20 inches (243.8 × 157.5 × 50.8 cm)

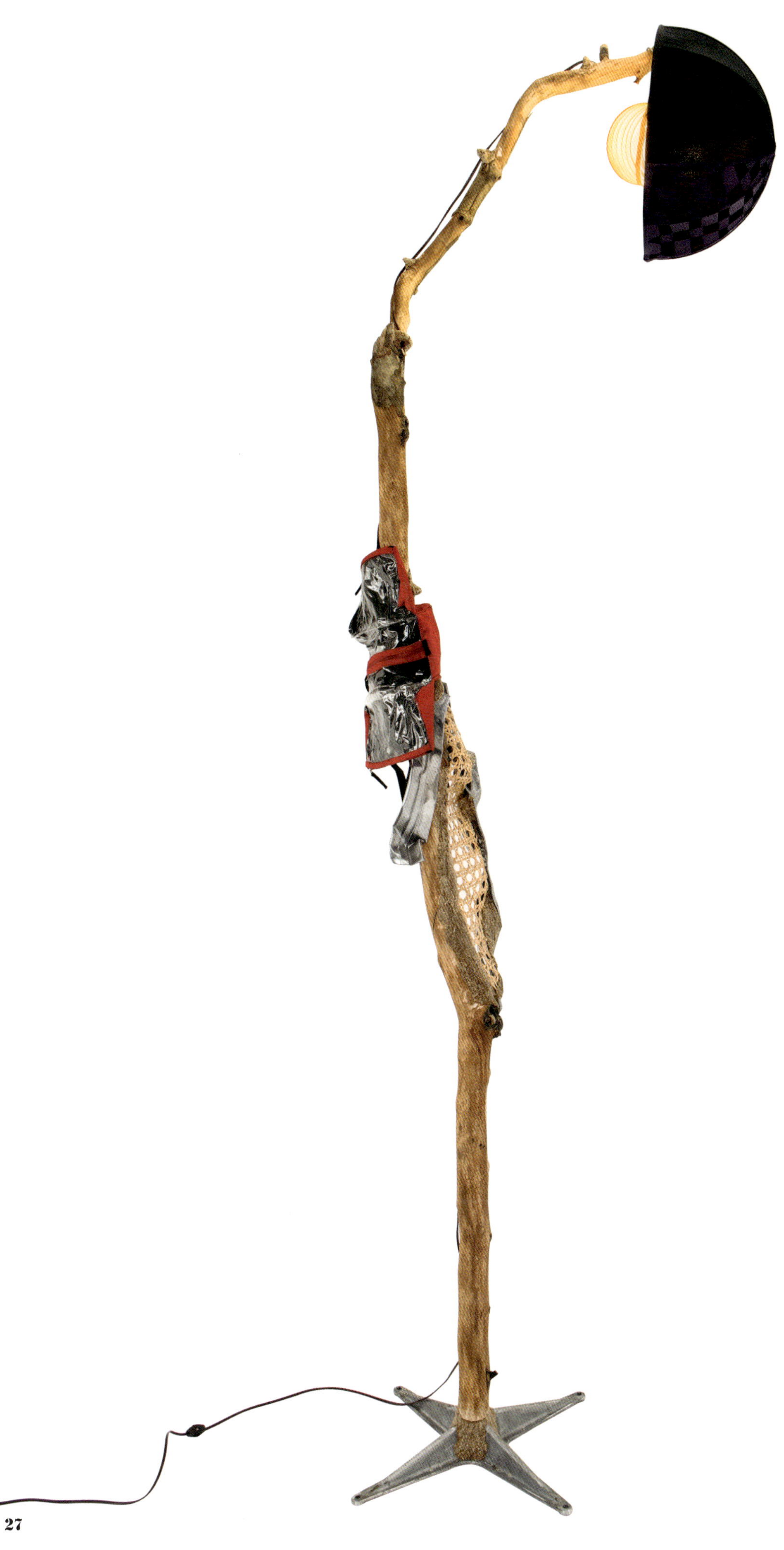

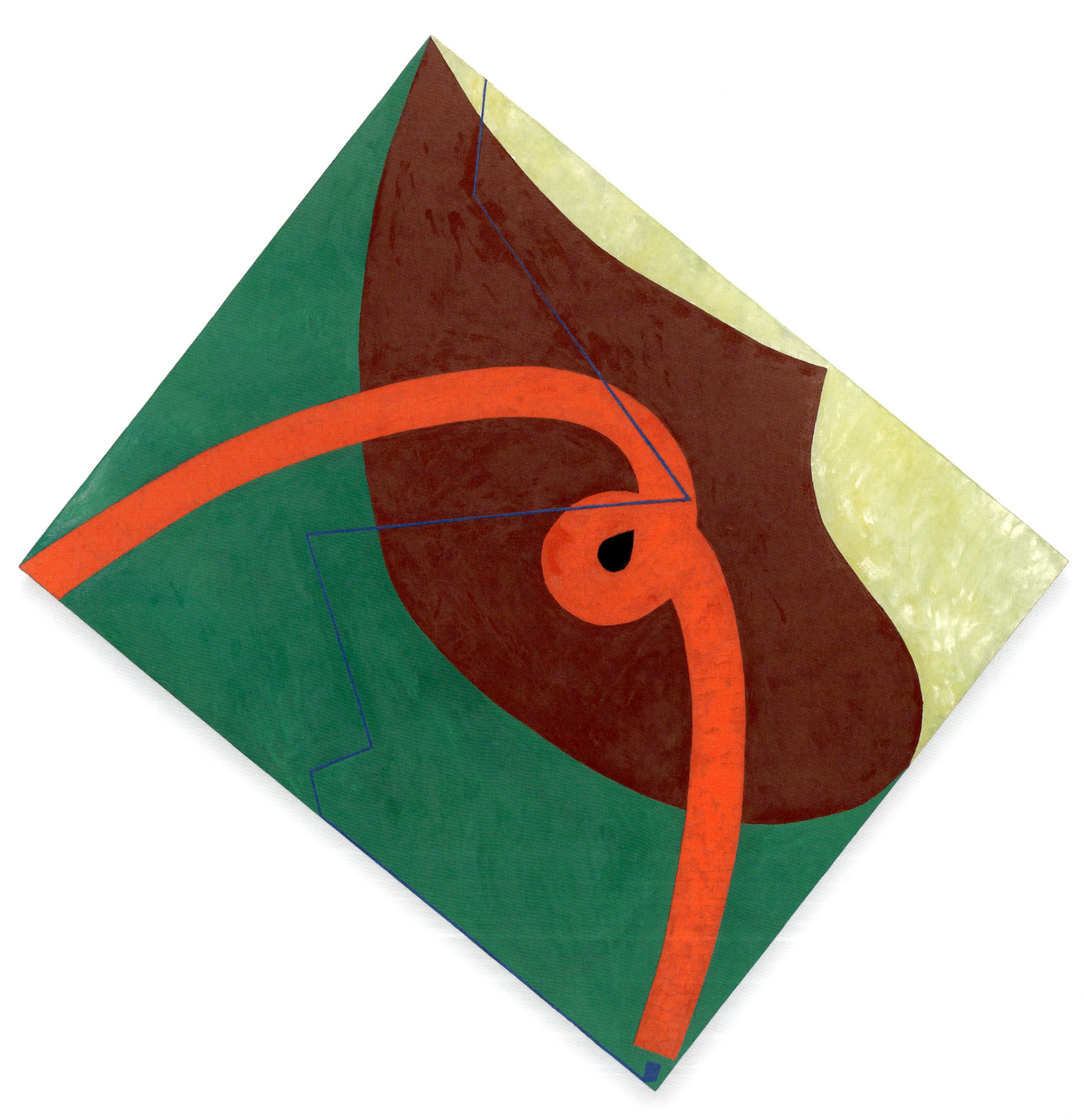

Elizabeth Murray, Falling, 1976
Oil on canvas
118 × 119 inches (299.7 × 302.3 cm)

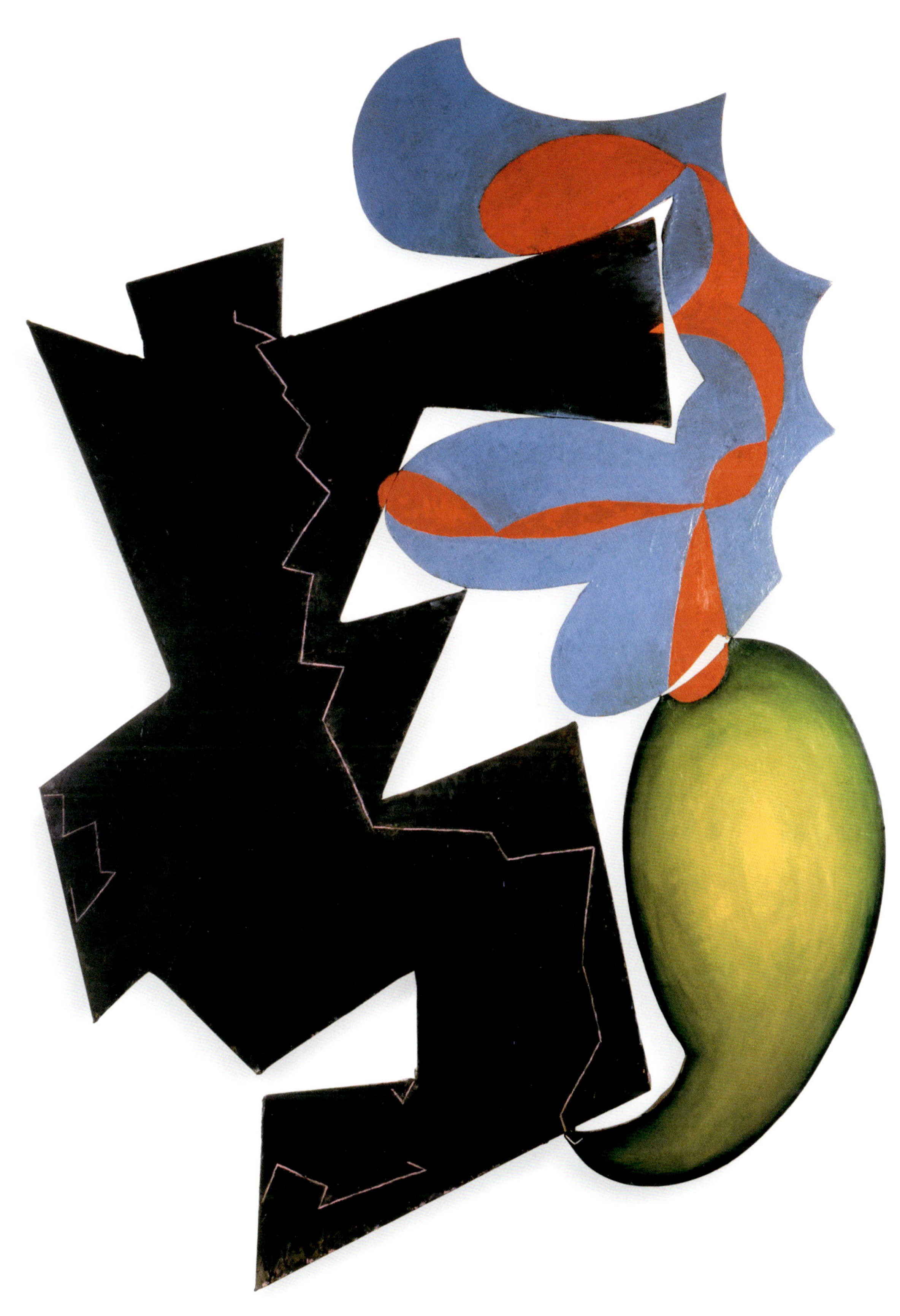

Elizabeth Murray, Sentimental Education, 1982
Oil on canvas
127 × 96 inches (322.6 × 243.8 cm)

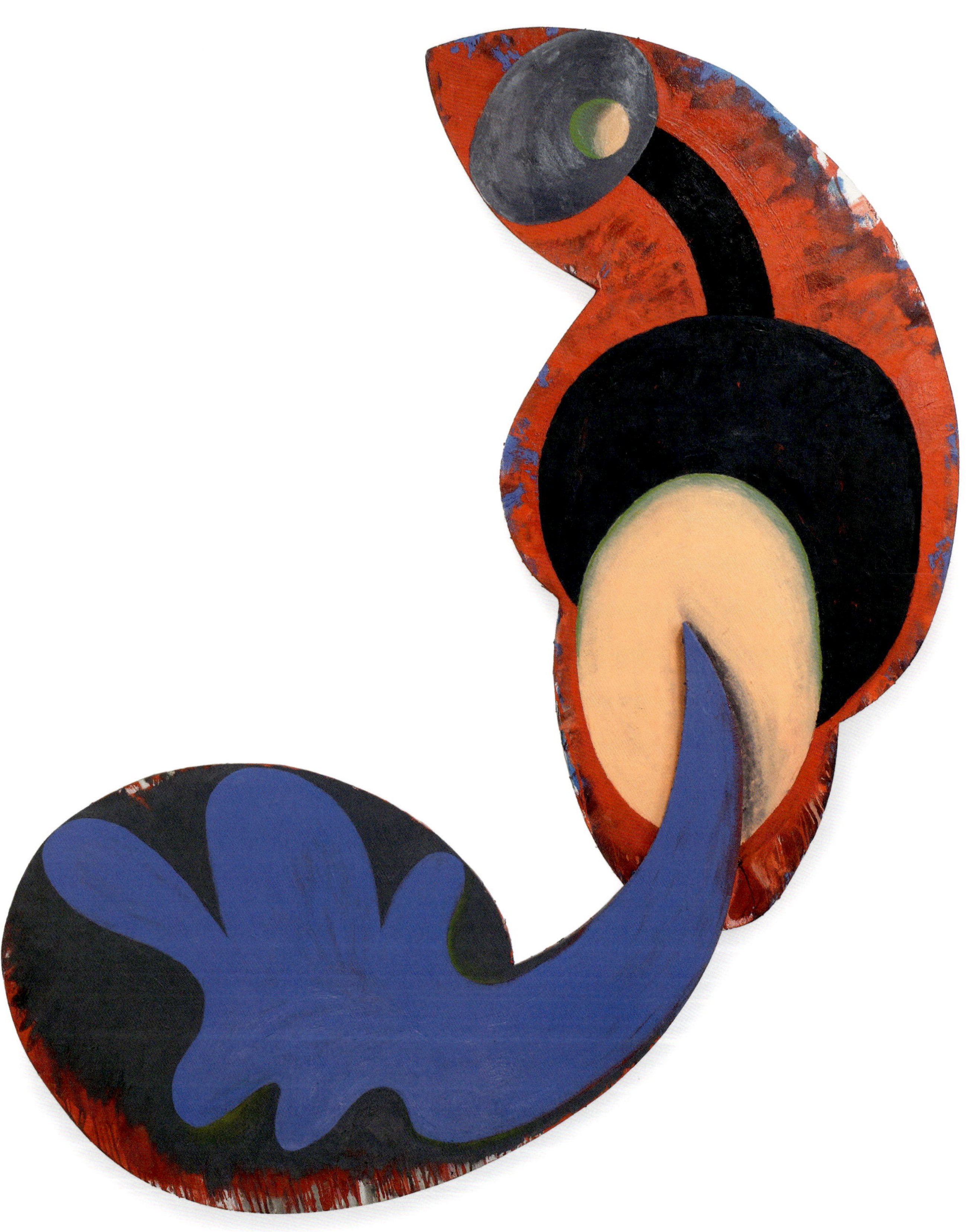

Elizabeth Murray, Fire Cup, 1982
Oil on canvas
95 × 78 inches (241.3 × 198.1 cm)

OPPOSITE
Jessi Reaves, Butter-egg-chair, 2015
Chromed steel and polyurethane foam
25 × 20 × 32 inches (63.5 × 50.8 × 81.3 cm)

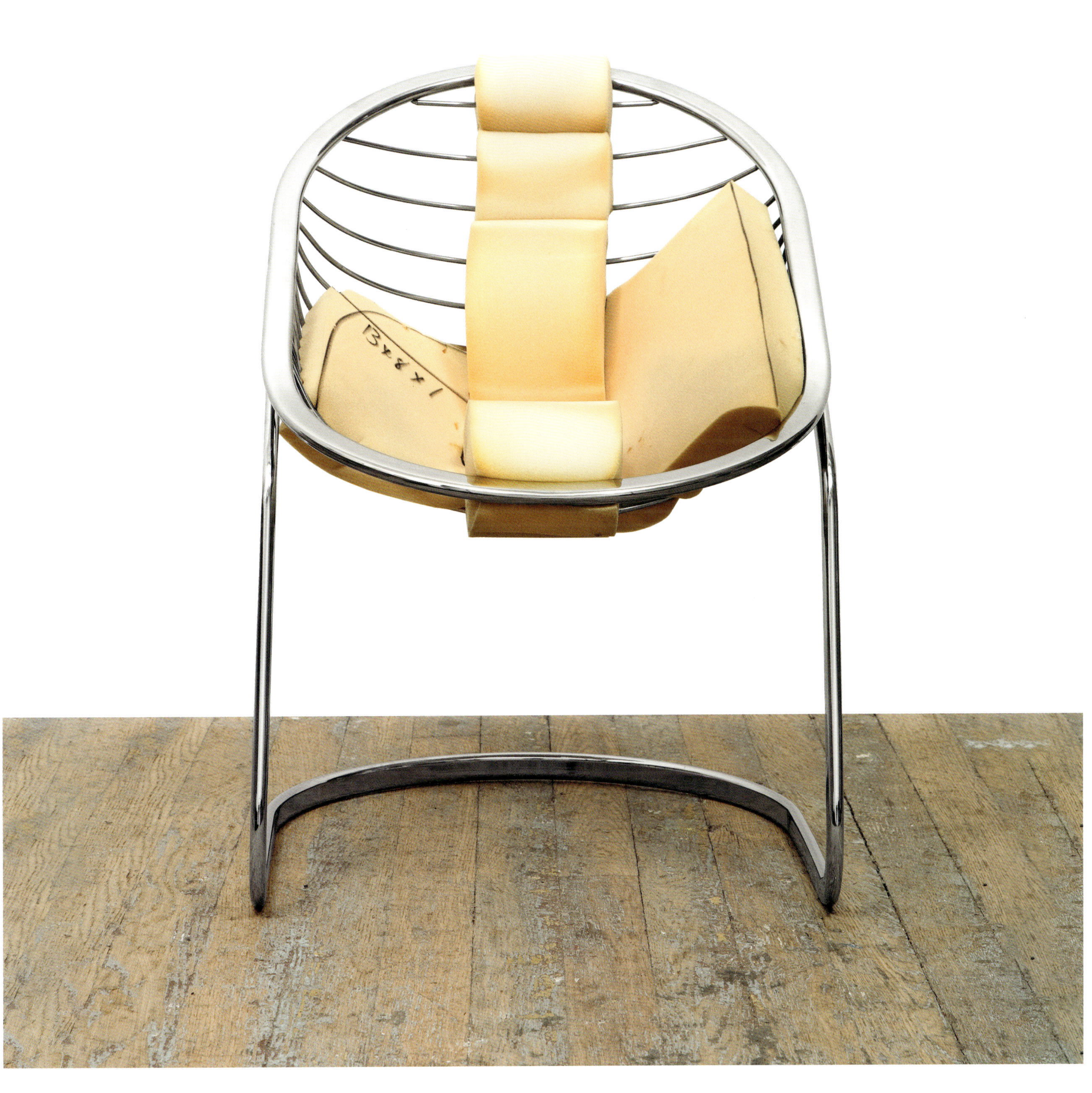
13x8x1

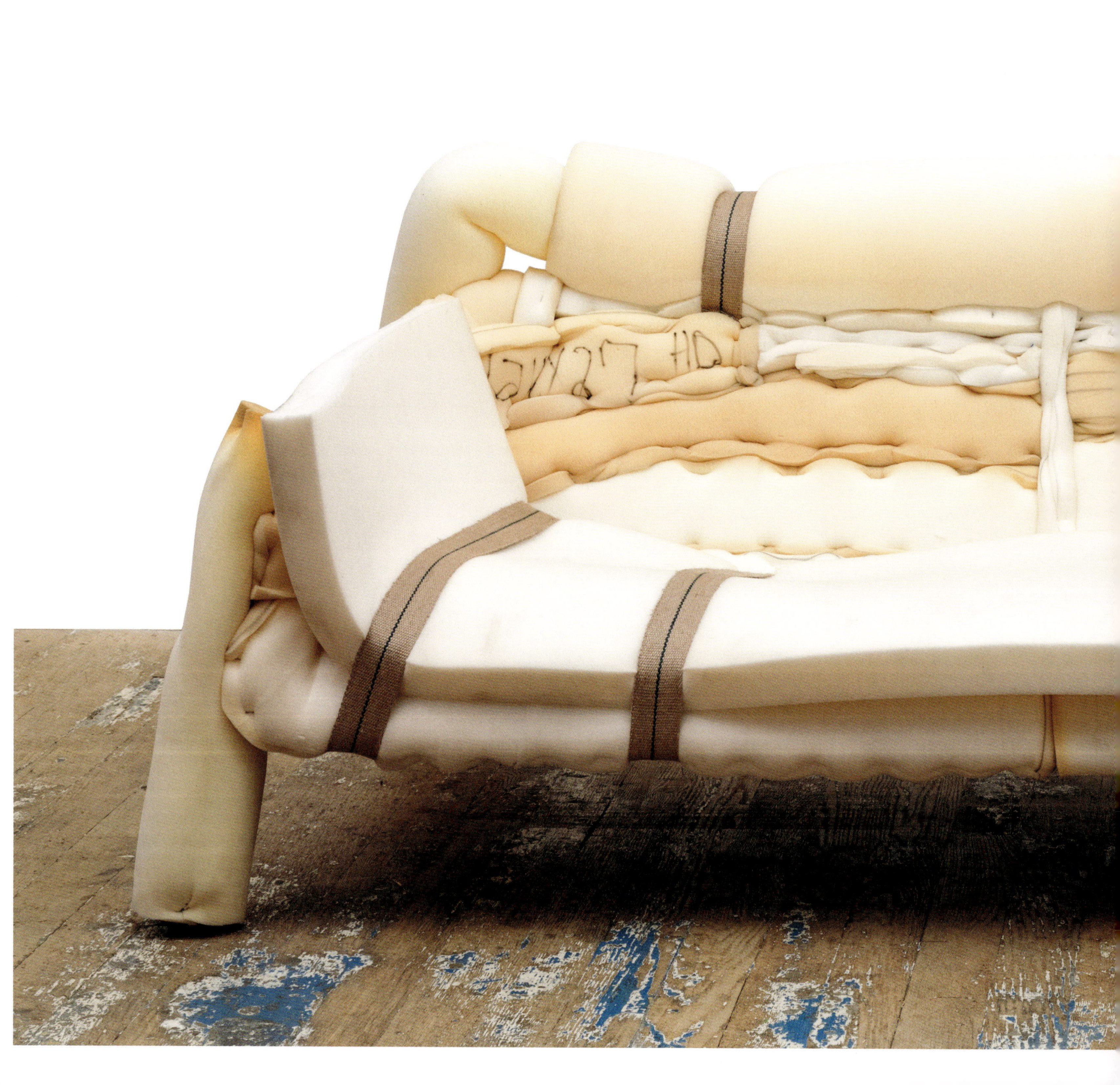

So I went to Chicago by myself in 1958, when I was eighteen. I knew about Leonardo da Vinci and Picasso and it all really threatened me so much.

When you got to the Art Institute, you chose fine art. How did that happen?

I was a teenage bobby-sox kid. I was putting three inches of make-up on and wearing crewneck sweaters and straight stuff like that. I went to Chicago thinking that I was going to be a commercial artist. But because I was so straight the most interesting people seemed to be the ones who were involved in painting and sculpture. So I was wearing my little Pendleton skirt, and I was being introduced to this incredibly free world where people were walking around with beards, and the men were not these jocks but were interested in reading poetry. And it seemed so incredible that people could make this stuff, art, and not care about money, not care about what other people thought about them. It was a totally different world from the kind of very straight Midwest thing I grew up in. And I got very involved in style as much as in the idea of being an artist.

When I finally decided that I was going to try to be a painter, I flipped out because all of a sudden--I guess I was twenty--I realized I had never decided anything on my own. And it was so difficult; it was very hard. I couldn't do it. I couldn't do the commercial art either. I couldn't draw a straight line--literally! I could not bear what one had to go through to make a layout. So that was a disaster. But still it was something I had planned to do from the time I was really little. It occurred to me that I don't have to do this, I could do something else.

I was there at the Art Institute and I was taking a painting class. So I started to try painting. It was enormously frustrating. I didn't know how all that stuff happened. I mean I had no idea. It sounds simplistic to say that we all have our destinies and I felt that something just kept leading me on. It was all so unknown. I was so frightened. So that made it even more important to get that work out for myself.

At that age and in a school situation you completely adopt the ideals of all the people around you: a fine artist was somebody who was really important, it was the real struggle, and it had intense meaning. Doing anything else was cheap in comparison. That whole heirarchy affected me a lot.

The other thing was looking, looking at the art in the museum. I saw all those paintings and I began to relate to them. It really never occurred to me that painting was something that was just about communication, it was that it had such a power to affect people visually. I began to just want to do it.

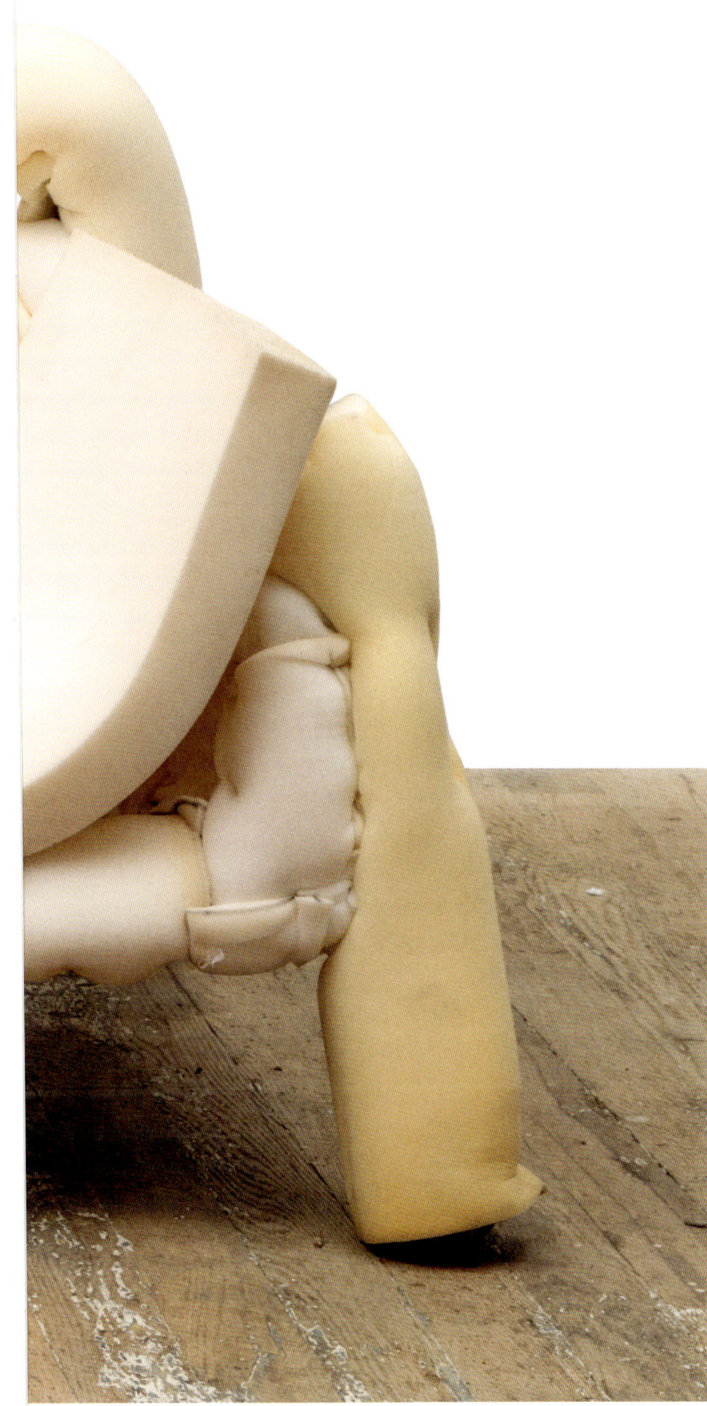

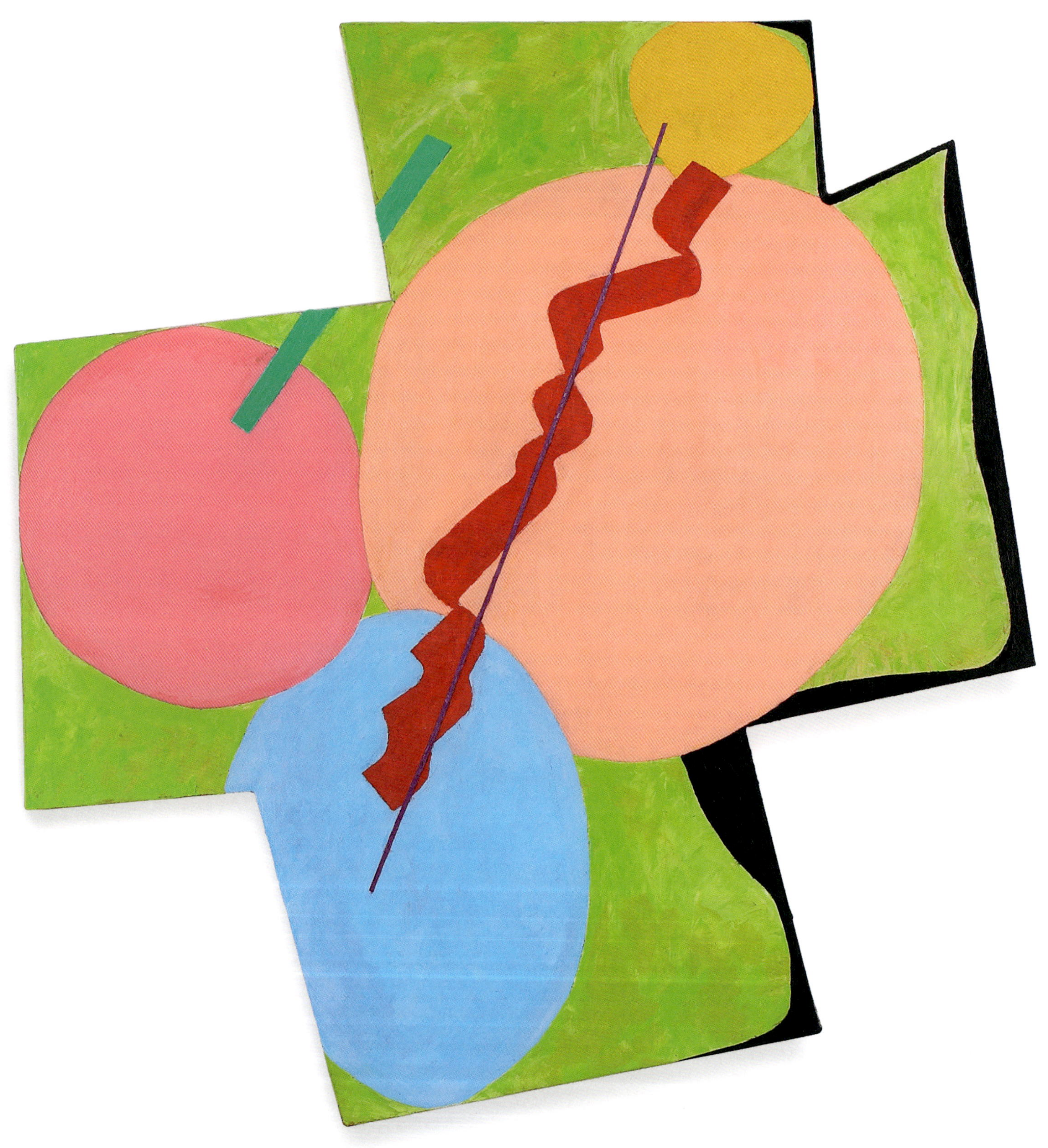

PREVIOUS SPREAD
Jessi Reaves, Foam Couch with Straps, 2016
Upholstery foam, fiberglass, wood, and webbing
29 × 77 × 35 inches (73.7 × 195.6 × 88.9 cm)

ABOVE
Elizabeth Murray, Twist of Fate, 1979
Oil on canvas
56 1/4 × 54 1/4 inches (142.9 × 137.8 cm)

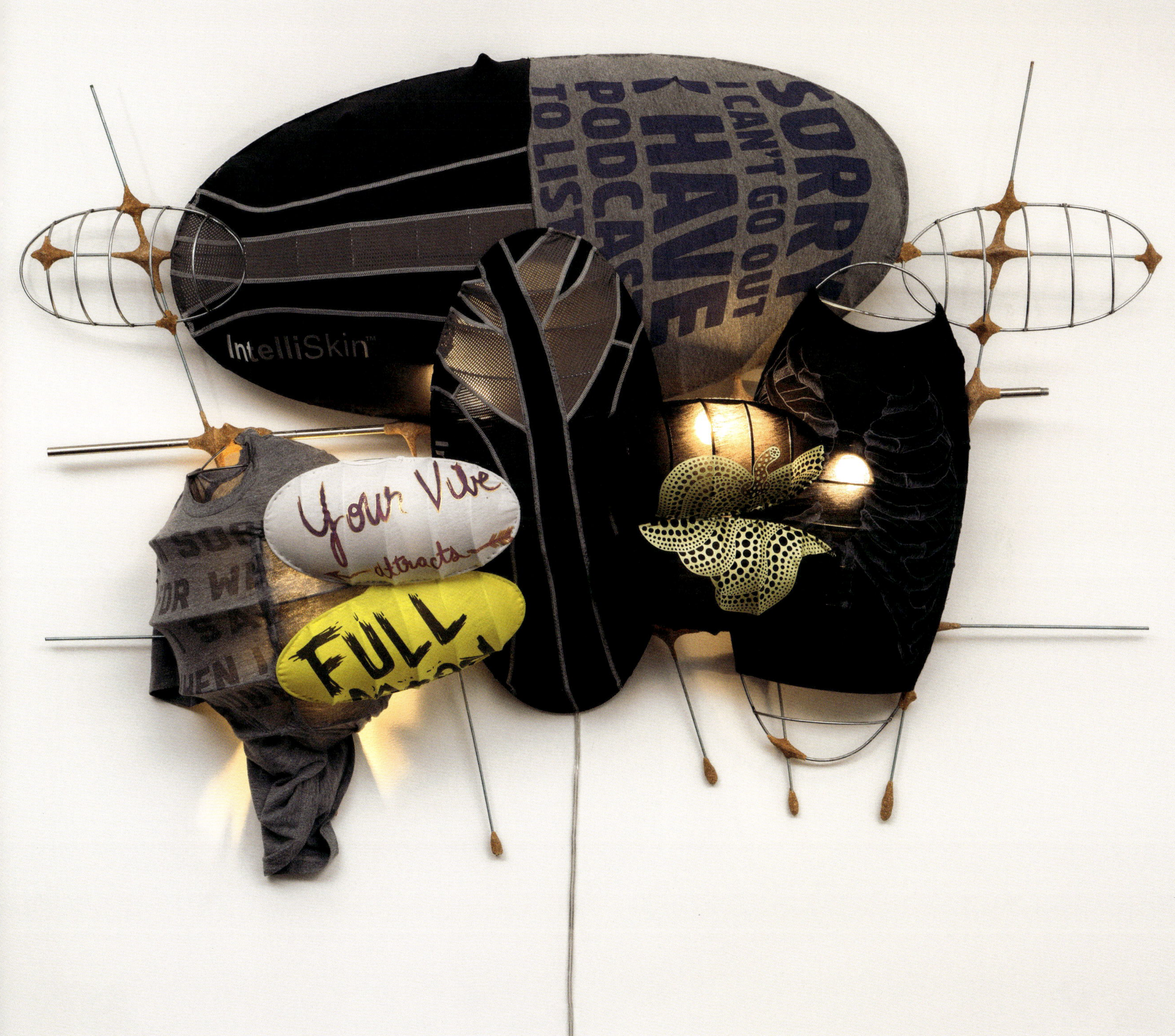

Jessi Reaves, Drive through the back of your eyes, 2019
Metal, fabric, sawdust, wood glue, and lamp wiring
40 × 56 × 8 inches (101.6 × 142.2 × 20.3 cm)

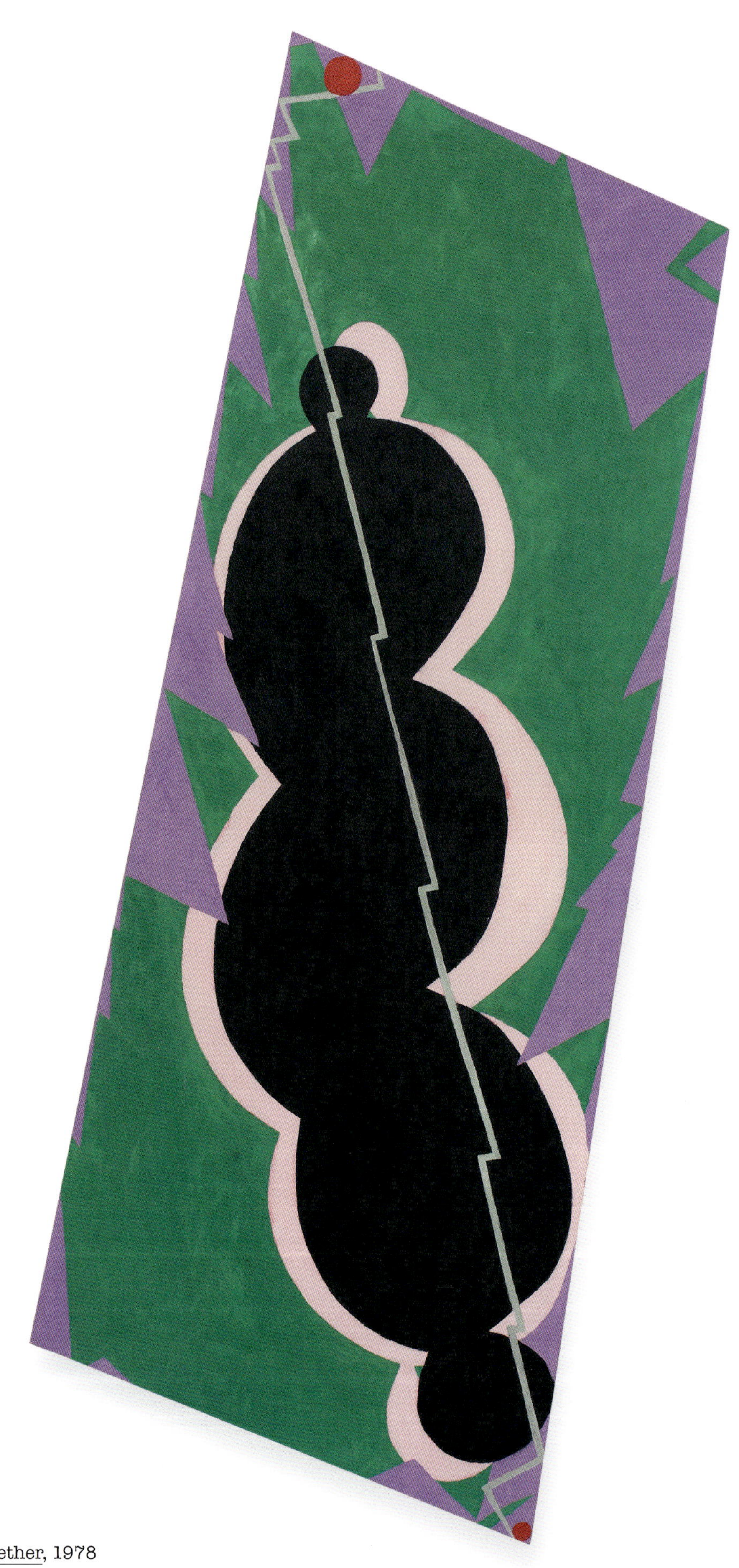

Elizabeth Murray, Parting and Together, 1978
Oil on canvas
123 × 63 inches (312.4 × 160 cm)

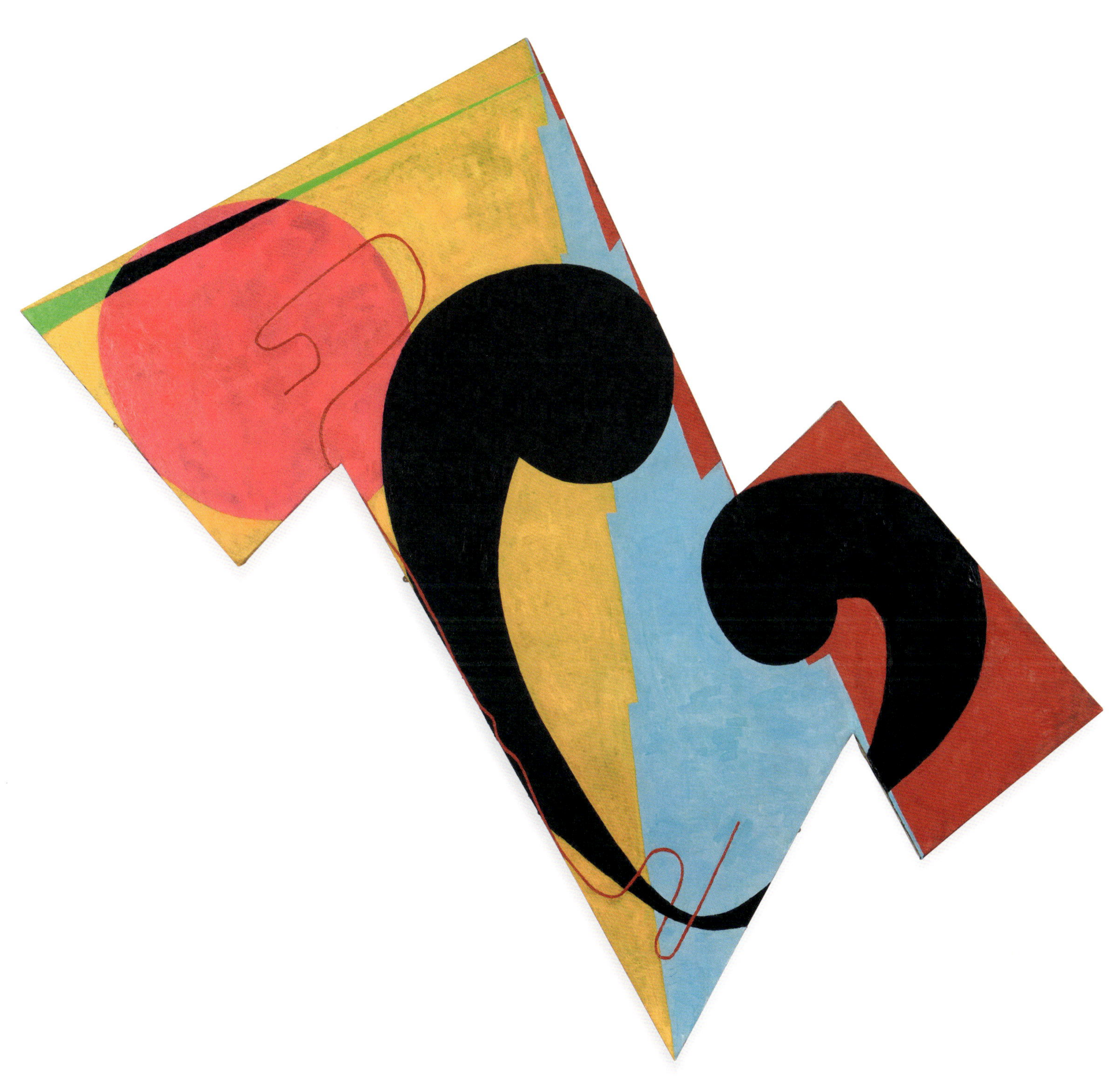

Elizabeth Murray, C Painting, 1980–81
Oil on canvas
109 × 114 inches (276.9 × 289.6 cm)
37

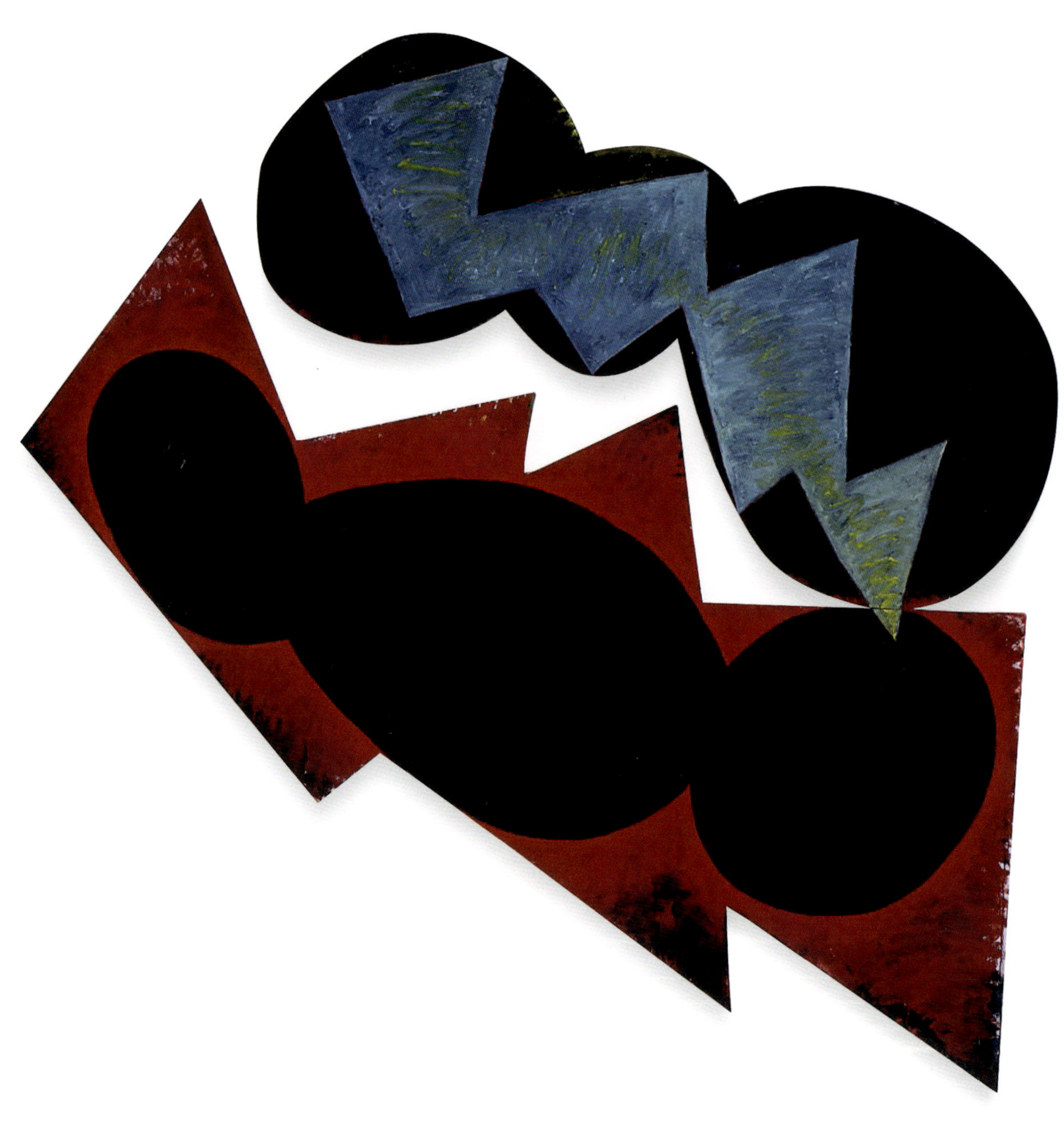

Elizabeth Murray, Heart and Mind, 1981
Oil on canvas
111 3/4 × 114 inches (283.8 × 289.6 cm)

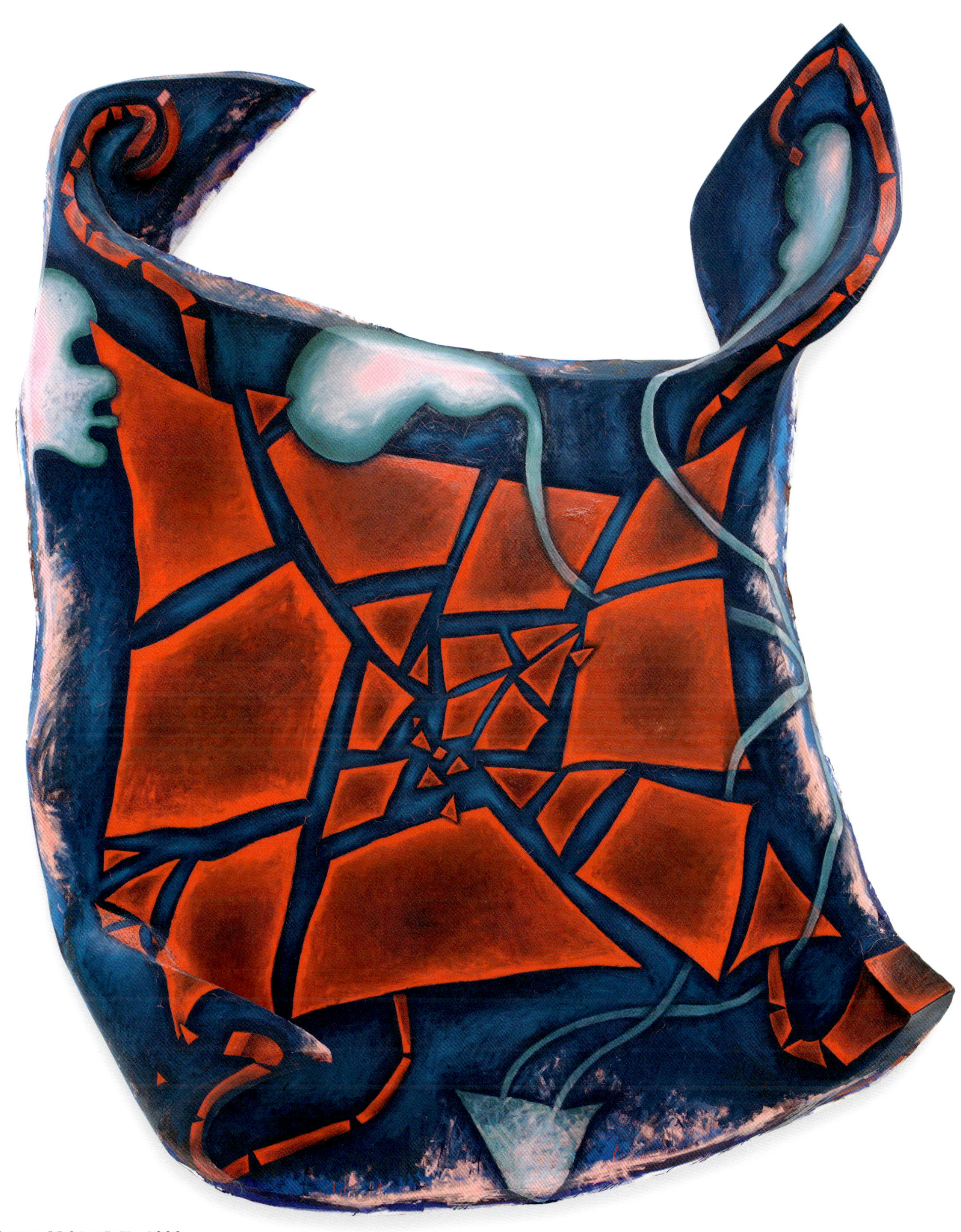

Elizabeth Murray, Making It Up, 1986
Oil on canvas on wood
124 1/8 × 95 1/8 × 16 inches (315.3 × 241.6 × 40.7 cm)

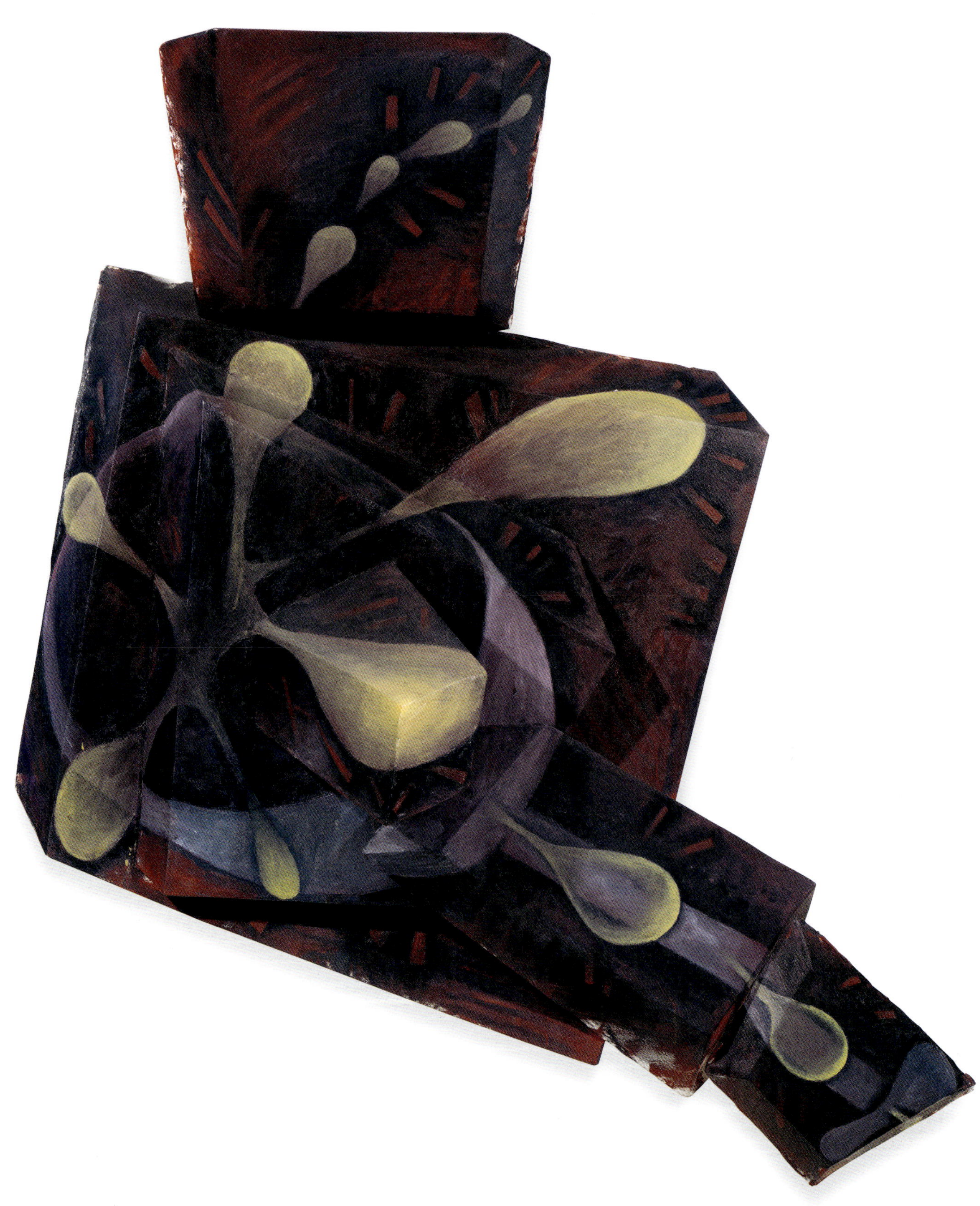

Elizabeth Murray, Wild Life, 1986
Oil on canvas
62 × 81 × 21 inches (157.5 × 205.7 × 53.3 cm)

OPPOSITE
Jessi Reaves, Twice Is Not Enough (Red to Green Chair), 2016
Wood, sawdust, steel, foam, silk, leather, and cotton
39 × 28 × 32 inches (99.1 × 71.1 × 81.3 cm)

So there was a certain kind of playfulness and a different kind of spirit about San Francisco. Did this have a direct effect on your work?

Yes it did. First of all, I started to work much, much larger. I started to work with more paint. And I got much more connected. It was a direction I was going in anyway. The work got more involved with images and then gradually more and more abstract and then back to images again. But at this time, I was very much affected by the Pop art show that came to L.A. It was the first time most of it had been seen in California. And there was a Jasper Johns show someplace in San Francisco.

I was very affected by the show of Johns, it was just fantastic. Watching someone use paint in such a structured kind of way and yet with that kind of humor and that kind of seriousness all combined, it all felt very pertinent to me and very psychological also. But it wasn't so klutzy as the Chicago stuff. I felt like there was more structure. It had a kind of formality to it and it laughed at formality at the same time.

I think it is important for me to feel--not that art has meaning, I think that is a given--but that it is communicating, it is reaching out in some very specific ways and commenting socially. And Pop art certainly did it. The paintings I ended up liking the most were the Oldenburgs. And, for a while, Warhol, but then he got too media-oriented for me. It was another way of looking at what art could be. I think it was a very open, exciting time. There was a lot going on then. Very different from now somehow.

What was your work like at Mills?

Big drippy paintings with surface kinds of forms. I was influenced by Gorky and de Kooning. It was real unconscious work. Very physical work. I was going up to the canvas and smushing the paint on and throwing it on. It was my whole life.

One really big thing that happened was that I met my friend Jennifer Bartlett there. And that has been a very important friendship in terms of our art making. We got ourselves through a very lonely place by connecting with each other. We have shared a lot.

So what were some of the steps that led up to your getting to New York? You didn't come directly after Mills.

No. I got married when I was in graduate school, and we stayed in San Francisco for another couple of years. Then I got my first teaching job at a place called Rosary Hill College in Buffalo,

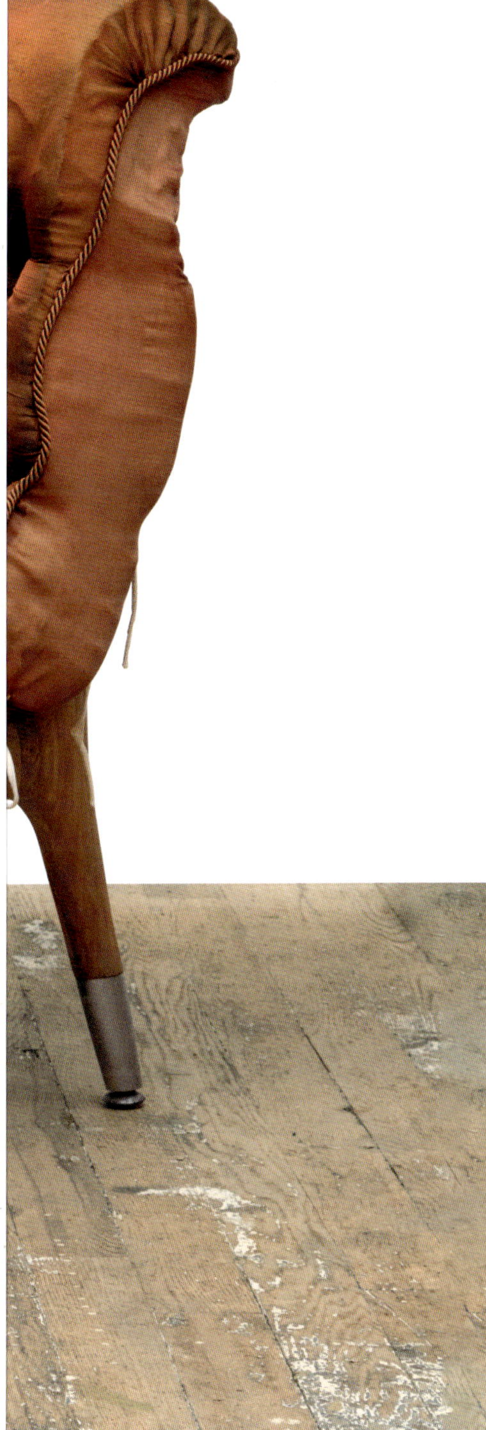

A CONVERSATION

The text that follows is an edited transcript of an audio-recorded interview that took place on October 29, 2019. Jessi Reaves is interviewed by Johanna Fateman at the artist's studio in Queens, New York.

Johanna Fateman
Jessi Reaves

Let's go back to the beginning. Can you give us a little background information? Where you came from, etc.?

I was born in northeast Portland. My parents moved to Oregon in the late seventies. My dad is an architect, so he was looking for a city that was just being built, because architects would be hired. Portland was growing and morphing at the time. My mom worked for the parks department; they have nice parks there. Eventually we moved to the suburbs, so I grew up near cute hobby farms and big Christmas tree farms, stuff like that.

And when did you start making art?

I'm not sure exactly, but I was young. My earliest memories are of making weird paper outfits—a combination of sewing and basic kids' crafts—stapling paper where there would be a seam. I would wear them until they would fall apart. Later, art was the only thing that I really excelled at, or that held my attention. I liked the social aspect of art. I liked that you could come in and out of what you were working on without too much effort; you could multitask. Think about high-school art class: you're sitting around and drawing and talking—I liked that. It was always easier for me to focus on two things at once. At home, I used to draw in front of the TV. There's something comforting about that. You're drawing while you're hearing something funny, and it pulls you out of yourself for a moment. Our TV was in a dark room, and we had a glass coffee table in there. I would put a lamp under the table and trace with it—an improvised light box. I would trace images from a kids' encyclopedia and other random books.

When did sculpture start for you?

I don't think I made sculpture on my own terms before I went to college. I went to Rhode Island School of Design and tried studying furniture design for a semester, but I clashed with the department. I hated the tediousness of the hand tools, and the focus was very much on traditional materials and the techniques of woodworking. All of the teachers were coming out of either the Studio Furniture Movement or product design. So it felt like there were two very rigid approaches to making things. I'm attracted to Studio Furniture from the 1980s and 1990s, but I found it bizarre how seriously they talked about that work. If you don't know Studio Furniture: it might be a record player that's also a carrot that's made out of some exotic zebrawood. It made me laugh, so I switched to painting.

I liked that my painting teachers were all working artists—Dike Blair, Carrie Moyer, and others who commuted from New York. The conversations in the painting department seemed more open and more conceptual. There were so many people making painting work from other materials. I started making sculptural paintings out of foam, sometimes from upholstery foam but mostly insulation foam, carved and painted or hung on the wall. Like carved reliefs with different objects inserted.

I sometimes regret not studying sculpture or not sticking with furniture to learn certain things, but at the time I just thought the painters were cool and I wanted to be like them. It's funny how, in Kate Horsfield's interview with her, Elizabeth Murray mentions how a fine artist seemed to her at that same age like someone important, someone who took risks and how she wound up adopting the ideals of the people around her. For me, it was mostly that, but I also felt intimidated by the amount of time it would take to learn the techniques of sculpture.

When did you graduate from RISD?

In 2009. Then I took a break from making art, somewhat. When I first moved to New York, I was living with six friends—a typical moving-to-New-York story. We had a big loft space, and we all had ambitions to make studios in the large open living room, but that never really came together. Moving to New York made me feel really insecure. I wasn't making art, because I was scared of making bad art, and I was floating around in a bad way, doing horrible side jobs.

Around 2012, I started taking little sewing jobs—making curtains and slipcovers and pillows—as well as poor-quality upholstery jobs. I didn't know how to do anything except basic sewing, I didn't know how to reinforce a seam or add a zipper; I just faked it. Then I started working for this guy who was making midcentury-modern-looking furniture. He worked with walnut and brass—hypermasculine, derivative, elevated, traditional materials. He was working on a chair that he wanted to have a "cool profile," and the way he talked about the elements of canonical design made an impression on me. Overhearing his opinion of what "mattered" gave me a lot to react to.

His uncle owned a building in the West Village, and he let me use the basement as a free studio while I was working on his projects. It was really very generous of him and special to have a free studio. For the first time, I was able to accumulate materials. I was able to make work, because that basement was like a depository for leftover stuff from other projects.

Can you tell me more about this guy's attitudes and what exactly you felt you were reacting to? How did that show up in your work?

I mean, it initially wasn't that clear to me, I just knew there was something generic about how he justified his tastes. But I did learn a lot from him: I would ask him why certain designs mattered to him, and he would indulge me with long explanations. I was really just trying to get paid, but I was soaking in this Brooklyn-woodworker environment at the same time. I think his obsessive reverence for modern design and his desire to fit into that lineage interested me. There were other funny things about it, too—like the fake sustainability of it all: a lot of the materials, like the leather, were sourced from an evil store in Midtown and glued with contact cement. It really piqued my interest in what design claims that it can or can't do. Which led me to certain other questions, like, who is design for? And why are people still obsessed with midcentury aesthetics? What does a taste for those things stand in for? What is pure or real?

I'm curious about that, too. The Noguchi table, which you've used in your work, is a good example of an enduring midcentury design. And even if your appropriation of it is irreverent in some sense, I would assume that you like that table and Noguchi's work generally. But maybe you don't?

I do like Noguchi, but that's not the point. I'm more curious about how that coffee table has come to represent other things. Also I'm curious about Noguchi as a sculptor who made furniture and lighting, and about how and why he kept those things separate. Obviously, in my own work, I call that distinction into question. On a basic level, I like that Noguchi coffee table. I've made what I call knockoff versions out of car fenders. Because automotive design changes quickly, there is always a new model or body style, and it's interesting to apply that to an enduring design. Most of the lampshade forms I work with are essentially made to look like reptilian, sliced-up versions of his Akari lamps.

I often choose recognizable furniture to use in my work because I want its history to be available to a close viewer, maximizing the potential content. I used to be interested in pulling things apart into smaller elements to scatter the readymade among multiple artworks. For my first show at Bridget Donahue's gallery, I took the leather off a Pervical Lafer sofa, then its frame, and then its legs. It was completely cannibalized and dispersed among various works. Now I'm more interested in keeping something together and building around it, letting the more subtle, dimensional aspects of the readymades dictate what happens.

I'm reminded—by your point about Noguchi keeping his art and design work distinct—that Duchamp's original definition of the readymade specified that the chosen (previously functional) object would become useless. But your art is functional, or semifunctional. It is meant to be used as furniture.

Right, I swing back and forth between appending the objects and obfuscating their use. There's no real particular process that I put them through. I just work on them until they feel like... like they are enough. How much my work feels like furniture versus how much it feels likes sculpture might have something to do with how much it adheres to or refers to the readymade. I want it to retain that information, but I also want it to veer off into its own psychodrama.

The first work that I ever saw of yours was in Bridget's office—a chair.

A big chair with stapled foam?

Yes, I didn't know about your work, and I was surprised to see someone sit in it.

People did love to sit in that chair. I think a big part of that was that they wanted to linger and talk to Bridget, and it was the only place to sit.

I'm anxious when I see people touch artworks; I'm worried that they aren't supposed to. Or I'm worried that I *am* supposed to, and I'm missing something by not interacting with it. That seems pretty fundamental to your work. That anxiety.

Yeah, I do like to play with that anxiety, but, like you described, it's kind of already there. When I got back into making art after taking that break, I was scared of making bad art and having to store it or look at it. I found it hard to justify making art for art's sake. That my sculptures had a functional potential propped them up somehow but also felt perverse, as though that was the one thing I knew I really shouldn't do.

Their functionality made art less of a decadent activity?

Sort of, but also the two aspects are always catching each other a little bit. I think, "Oh, if it fails as a sculpture, then it could succeed as a chair." That foam chair was only accidentally comfortable. I had seen some painted animal chairs built by the artist Sven Lukin—he had them in his house. The sides of the chairs were thick, painted cutouts of tigers, which were spanned by the seats and backs. It was such a simple way to make a chair. So I built the frame of Bridget's chair out of plywood and randomly placed the seat and the back—I may have looked up the average seat height. And the foam—those were scraps I had from upholstery projects. I just started stapling it on to cover the surface. In upholstery, you never want to see the staples, and you don't expose the foam. I realized the potential of that material to make people uneasy when I showed people that chair, and they saw that to sit in it they would have to come into direct contact with the foam. It's hard to find out what a material can do until you put it into action.

Yeah, why is foam so disgusting, do you think? I guess because it's unwashable.

It's unwashable, and it's like Velcro. Hair clings to it. That chair would get so dirty. And it had a little ottoman, and people would put their feet up on it. It also feels vulnerable—the foam should be concealed, protected. That thing was really filthy, and was changing color. It was falling apart right in front of you.

Part of what is so cool and perplexing about your work is that it shows someone doing the techniques "wrong"—but not completely wrong. Skill-wise, your work occupies a gray area.

I like the results that come from working with what you have lying around. For example, I may have a loose awareness of the right way to do something, but I want to keep my work out of the realm of specialty woodworking or elevated craft. I don't want my studio to be a woodshop. Using modified or very basic tools helps keep things loose. I have what I call garage-dad tools, I like that they are compact and approachable. I like my work to feel like anyone could have made it in their own garage, but maybe while in a terrible mood. If I had a drill press, for example, it would make some tasks simpler, but I don't want a tool like that to infuse my work with its seriousness. So instead things wind up crooked, but I figure out my own ways to make the connections look the way I want them to.

There's an interesting part of the Murray interview where she is talking about making sculptures. She says that she "was interested in doing sculpture that was painted, that was kinetic, that moved, that you could sit on, that was soft, that was hard." She goes on to describe how they were "totally impossible." And she realized that for those sculptures to work they would have to be fabricated by someone else.

I've only seen a few of her sculptures, have you seen *Red Shoe* [1996]? I don't know if she fabricated it. I was really surprised by that image. It sits outdoors and it's very heavy-handed. It looks like it was carved out of cedar, or some squishy wood that would crack and split apart over time.

I don't know, but it sounds like she didn't end up having things fabricated in general, because, as she continues in the interview, "to make those pieces work I needed to have things made outside of the studio... and that took money that I didn't have. Also fabricated for me meant less contact. It was very clear that I needed to have that contact."

I feel the same way. I also want as much contact as possible. I've recently figured out a way to incorporate fabrication into my work, though. I'll have certain larger elements made for me, but I'm conscious of the way they enter the studio. I think of them as readymades, and I don't control the process too much. I kind of just go along with what the fabricator wants to do. I say, "Build this the way it makes sense to you." For example, the frames for the ottomans eventually became really large and cumbersome, and I decided that it isn't that important that I build the forms, because I end up having enough contact as I work on them. I look at things I find randomly on the sidewalk, things I've sought out specifically and things I've had fabricated all in the same way. I need to be able to say, "I can cut this in half if I need to."

The cost is a very real part of that for me, too: I try not to use expensive techniques that tend toward inflexibility and precision, and I work with people who know how to build things. I want to be able to change my mind. My materials can't feel too precious.

So would you say your process is spontaneous?

Yes, because I'm pretty emotional at the studio and because I tend to work in big bursts. I'll set one thing on top of another, for example, and leave them there. If I haven't moved them after a few weeks, it might mean that it is worth pursuing. I'll have another burst of activity, where I figure out what the connection is and maybe I start to cement them together. I don't plot things out ahead of time. Making drawings usually comes later on. Lately I'm not even seeking out particular objects. The things I want to work with seem to wind up in the studio, so it's just about showing up every day and working through ideas.

How do materials wind up here?

I have friends who bring me things. I'm very lucky to have people looking out for me in that way. For one sculpture I'm working on now, I'm using little wooden salad bowls. I don't exactly know how my friend Andy knew I would want them. Probably because I like wooden things from the seventies. My assistant, Thomas, is a runner; he goes on long runs in Brooklyn, and when he sees something good he sends a picture and I rush to go get it. I also spend a lot of time looking without knowing exactly what I'm looking for, just generally looking. I like the flea market on West Twenty-Fifth Street in Manhattan and random others in the neighborhood here in Queens. And eBay, of course.

For a while I was working with the Cesca chair, which is easy to find broken on the street or in a thrift store, so I just piled them up in the corner, and eventually I started to work on that stack of chairs as a shelf. I like that chair because it was designed to be ubiquitous. It was in every household and part of daily life. But it's almost like the wooden salad bowl and the chair have gone in opposite directions: the chair has become a coveted design object, and the bowls have become garbage. To buy and use them seem almost disgusting.

They are associated with a bygone, "earthy" counterculture, I guess.

That's part of the appeal of a lot of wooden objects. Nobody wants them—so they're accessible—but they hold a certain kind of information about the world. Most people in my parents' generation had a craft. It was common for people to build practical little things, just for fun. It was entertainment that was related to an ethic of sustainability—like growing your own food. My mom did macramé; sometimes she would make plant holders, but other times it was a huge tapestry from a pattern she would follow in a book. It was strange because it got close to art, but it wasn't that personal. Of course, culture dramatically went in another direction, so these salad bowls are like souvenirs from a different way of thinking.

To me, your salad bowls exemplify the perversity of your work: you are purposely misunderstanding their function. Your logic is that they're wooden and so is furniture, so it makes sense to make them into furniture. But of course that's very weird.

It is weird, but they do feel very close to furniture; they're used and made of the same material. I'm also using the bowls and other similar things because they are low on the totem pole in terms of design objects. I like insisting on their importance by giving them a different function. Putting the salad bowl under the glass as a support traps the functionality of the bowl and freezes it. Certain types of objects get sucked up into an obsession with taste and that brings them closer to the realm of art. I like messing with the hierarchy of what is collected and elevated.

There's sometimes a darkness to your work, I think, which is not necessarily from your process, but because used furniture, used stuff has an aura—it's been in someone's house, absorbing their history. You wonder what happened to that person?

Sometimes furniture is overtly psychological in a way that annoys me, like when it feels so extremely Freudian that it's just over the top, like "Grandpa used to sit here every day. . . ." But I do want to borrow some of that darkness, or play with its potential. One of the darkest pieces I've made is called Brown Cabinet [2017], and it has a painting of a demon on the back. I had remembered how we used to have these split wooden doors in my house, a type of door where the wood grain is mirrored down the middle. I would always see faces in the wood because it was symmetrical, like the face of an old man with a long beard. But they got me thinking about different ways furniture and materials have a certain darkness. With that piece I was telling myself a story about how this cabinet might be in your house—it's weird and pushed up against the wall—and then one day you pull it out from the wall, and there is this creepy demon face on the back, and its just like, "Wow, I was living with this the whole time." I don't think the work is about that narrative—it's just there for me. It helps me. Even ways that painted furniture can be about something beyond adornment.

With both upholstery and assemblage there are junctures—I'm interested in questions of when to show them and when to expend energy concealing them. When I make a "new" work, I don't aspire to pristine surfaces, manufactured surfaces. There is a fear of blemish that steers us toward serial modes of production and fabrication.

And the sculptures that have lives as furniture will continue to be worn, scratched, and degraded with use. I don't know if you have an all-encompassing policy about your work: is everything touchable or useable, or are only some pieces?

I wish they were more touchable, but it's hard to regulate. I don't want to control what people do or don't do. I don't want to say, "Use it like this," and I don't like long explanations about how you should sit. Nothing annoys me more than signage that says, "Please touch the art." I feel like the people who need to touch it, or who are curious enough to sit, or ask to sit, will wind up doing it. Otherwise they can just imagine how they might use it.

Do collectors who have your works in their homes use them? For example, has someone bought one of your shelves and then put a few of their own things on it?

Yes. I've gotten some pictures of things being used in homes. I try not to linger too long on those images. The shelves are funny. They might be a special case, because they're on the wall. I've seen one of my shelves installed in someone's house with nothing kept on it. I had one of the first shelves I made at my apartment for a long time—I kept lotions and cosmetics on it, and I enjoyed using it. I like that they will hopefully be used to varying degrees among different people.

At the 2017 Whitney Biennial people were sitting on your couches, of course. How did they hold up?

They didn't hold up well at all. By the end of the show, I was going every week to repair them. I learned a lot from that exhibition in terms of what happens to certain fabrics under extreme conditions. It was like, you leave your house wearing a dress to go to a party, but instead you wind up on a road trip for three months wearing only that same dress. That's what it looked like after every weekend.

What was frustrating was that those sofas were almost too generous in terms of seating; they were too functional. During museum hours, they were covered with people, so I felt like you couldn't see much of them. I had never shown anything in a museum, or anywhere near that scale. I don't think I could have anticipated what was going to happen to them, and it was a struggle to keep them up to my standards as they continued to change. But I did enjoy going to the museum early in the morning, before they would open, and just being in the show, sewing my little thing. Getting to see the bigger scope of what it takes to maintain that type of exhibition.

Have you done that, or would you do that, for collectors?

It's hard to say, generally. I'm open to repairing things, but I'm also open to seeing how other people would repair them. There's no guarantee that I will repair them.

You choose great titles for your works. Do you use them to underscore their hybrid status as furniture/artwork?

Thank you! I really enjoy titling my work, I think it's another opportunity to double down on certain aspects. Sometimes I am being strategic, like, "I need to have *shelf* in the title." Just to put the piece where I want it to be. I like insisting on what something is, and the title is a way to do that.

I keep a running list of titles that usually come from whatever I'm reading. Sometimes I name them for jokes I have with myself. I've never wanted to use *Untitled*; I always feel disappointed when I see it. I know there are people who have done interesting things with *Untitled*, but I like to make a statement—for humor's sake, or to attach something concretely personal to the object. I admire Murray for doing that. Some of her titles are so personal they almost make you cringe. I wonder about her painting *Don't Be Cruel* [1985–86]. It has a dark palette and a crack through the center, and then that name on top if it.... You know something was going on with her!

I have a great book of her work. Each page has one painting, with the title and a short paragraph she wrote about the work on the facing page. She includes practical, personal, and compositional things like, "This is the first time I put a hole in the middle of a painting." And then sometimes she refers to them emotionally, like, "This is about when I met my husband." It's nice to read an artist's own words about their work, and the title is a quick way to get some of that.

So, let's talk about Murray, about this particular, upcoming show where your work will be shown alongside hers. What do you think about it? What is your relationship to her art?

The first time I saw her work was in Chicago, when I was moving to New York. We stopped at the Art Institute of Chicago. There was an aggression to her paintings there that appealed to me. Some of them seemed to peel off the wall like roadkill. I felt they they were really arrogant in terms of how they took up space—not just wall space but how they jut out into the room. Following that, I've collected books of her work. Periodically looking at them has certainly influenced my own work.

When I started making wall works, which are shelves, I went to look at her work again. I was looking at how the shapes felt on the wall. I hadn't noticed the domestic or furniture objects in her work—that took me a while to see. I had started making shelves on the wall in part because I needed space to work on several things at once. But they got really thick, sticking out from the wall two or three feet. Maybe being more familiar with her work gave me a certain permission to do that.

Looking at even the thumbnail images of her work on the exhibition checklist, you can see formal similarities between your work and hers, but what effect do you think the presence of your "furniture" will have on how we perceive her paintings—will they read a little more as decor?

I don't think so. Her paintings seem to fight pretty hard against the purely decorative. I'm more interested in the potential that my work can prolong viewing. A few years ago, I was in a chaotic group show at Bed-Stuy Love Affair with something like fifty artists in it. I gave them that giant chair—the one you saw in Bridget's office—for the show. I would walk by the gallery and see people sitting in it, watching the one video work in the show. That really struck me. I hadn't considered how that chair might change the feeling of the show in terms of time spent looking. I do hope that will happen with this show. I hope the ottomans and other seating keep people there longer. Murray's paintings are bold, and maybe you feel like you "get" them at a glance, but I think the longer you look at them the more you see.

I hadn't thought of that. Will this show, in terms of your part of it, be mostly seating?

It will be a mix. There will be ottomans, which will play with the blankness of museum furniture. And I'm hoping to build a carpeted platform; the space has a diamond shape, and there is very large and prominent ductwork in the corners. So the "sunken living room" will kind of curve around that. There are a few of Murray's paintings that resemble cartoon machines, like you put one thing in and it goes through a process to come out the other side as something else. I think it would be good to play with the feeling of the ductwork like that in the space.

A platform like the one in your 2019 show at Bridget Donahue's gallery?

Yes, similar. That was meant to be a sunken living room, but because of its layout in the space it became more like a little amphitheater! My friend Brad called it "the quad." I didn't see that form in the DNA of the sunken living room, though of course it's there. It is a classical congregation space. It was perhaps a bad idea to begin with. I was thinking about how to have seating in the space without chairs and then how could I stretch it out and morph it into a platform for other works. And it divided the space in half. There will be certain chairs at CAMH that you can't sit on. So that tension of "you can sit on this, and you can't sit on that" will come into play.

Might the defamiliarization of the domestic be a theme common to your work and Murray's?

I like that comparison. Like I said, it took me a long time to see the domestic objects in her work—to even spot the cups, or to realize that some of her paintings are in fact views of tables from above, with the legs spiraling upward and outward. But they do force you to see these very familiar things in a new way, which is maybe parallel to my work.

Kate Horsfield asks Murray about how people read bodies and natural forms and sexuality into her work.

I also get a lot of anthropomorphic readings of my work, which I'm wary of. The blemished surface, as we talked about earlier, is one of the more interesting ways in which my work relates to the body.

Do you think your works are sexual?

I do—although I would say, like Murray, that maybe that's just part of me, so it's part of the work. It's reflected in something as rudimentary as how the different elements fit together. I think sexuality is tied up, in fascinating ways, in the era of modern design I'm often engaging with. Over the summer, I was reading Paul B. Preciado's *Pornotopia*, which is about *Playboy*'s influence as a design magazine. *Playboy* advocated for International Style from its inception. They were promoting a vision for a kind of erotic utopia, and trying to define the need for a new, masculine notion of domestic space during the Cold War era. I became especially fascinated by Hugh Hefner's bed. He designed it so it was a whole working-living system, which included a refrigerator and a television. He would lay out the whole magazine in bed. His activities together with all this technology were part of a new, multimedia sexual sphere. In my mind, design and masculinity have always been completely entangled, but that book helped me understand why those associations are so strong.

It's provocative to think of modern design as regendering interior space, though things are never so clear-cut. I know that Murray's cups and tables are read in terms of the "home," but they seem equally engaged with the not-feminine, painterly tradition of the still life.

Right. I think that's all about perspective. She kind of upends the point of view of the still life. It's like an Alice-in-Wonderland distortion of a table, or maybe it's like staring down into the bottom of a cup for so long that you forget what you're looking at.

But, yeah, men also live in houses; they use cups, too! Before you got here I was reading an essay Carroll Dunham wrote in 2005 about Murray for *Artforum*, in which he says:

> The often-invoked theme of "domesticity" coexists with her formal explorations, and it recedes when we remember, as Francine Prose beautifully remarked about Murray's work, "the (one would think) self-evident fact that the domestic *is* the world." By locating her subjects firmly within the zone of hearth, home, and studio, Murray has maintained a steady pressure on her audience to acknowledge the quotidian realities that circumscribe any life and are only rarely foregrounded in painting at her level. And besides, none of the male artists mentioned here (with the possible exception of [Peter] Saul, who almost insists on it) has ever had his work analyzed, at least in print, as a function of being a white man of a certain age, and until such a discourse becomes comfortable we will remain stuck in our cultural adolescence.

I love that. So, in making furniture, do you feel are you entering the "masculine" sphere? Or desecrating it through your use of design objects or furniture?

How I think about that has shifted. I'm kind of all over the place with it at any given moment, maybe because I'm attracted to that type of contradiction? In the studio, I am pretty destructive, I enjoy the process of disassembling or disemboweling things that people have a lot of passion and reverence for. That is certainly a part of my practice. Sometimes people give me really nice things, and I am susceptible to obsessing over them as design objects. But I try to keep away from that and instead channel a kind of adolescent energy where nothing is too precious. Sometimes I feel like I'm trying to get to a weird state of mind, like I'm a teenager making over my bedroom and choosing a new identity at random but then getting distracted halfway through so it's never fully formed.

The conversation with Murray ends with her talking about the importance of art at that moment, in terms of the political climate. She doesn't reference anything specifically, but I assume her alarm and despair are in reaction to the Reagan era—the country's swing to the right, the ascendance of Christian conservatism, and the administration's budget cuts to the National Endowment for the Arts. She says, "It is not an accident that one of the first things that every repressive regime does, like the Nazis, is to get rid of the art."

Her reaction to the politics of that moment is interesting and certainly still relevant. I know politics will always play a role in my work, whether I want it to or not. I graduated from college in 2009, and in a certain way the economic downturn relieved any immediate pressure on me having a career. It was nearly impossible to get a job, so I didn't have to feel like a huge failure when I couldn't get anything going. We all had sympathy for each other. In the past, it might have been easier to move to New York and work for a magazine or a gallery or at some other art-adjacent day job—but that was harder in 2009. Looking back I'm really grateful for that lack of pressure and—in a way—the atmosphere of hopelessness of that moment. I know I'm speaking narrowly about the recession, but I think there is a certain freedom to moments that lack prosperity.

It also made me interested in the relationship between money and politics in a way that I hadn't been before. We are still digging into those ideas now. I listen to public radio a lot when I'm in the studio, so politics is sometimes literally in the air. Of course, the 2016 election was very emotional. I was in the studio hearing it all unfold. I felt misled and disappointed. But I think one of the takeaways for me is that I'm just very distrustful of prosperity and success. That might seem obvious or unrelated, but I think the whole concept of "success" looks uglier and uglier. Like, what are we giving up in order to have all this prosperity? It seems like a lot is lost along the way. All things considered, it's a fairly good time to be an artist. It seems like a lot of other industries want to be connected to art; a certain type of artist is really celebrated in this moment. Unfortunately that is often the type of artist who is driven by success as an ultimate goal. I don't think art in general is being threatened. It's more like nuance and authenticity are slowly going extinct, which puts a kind of slimy film over a lot of it.

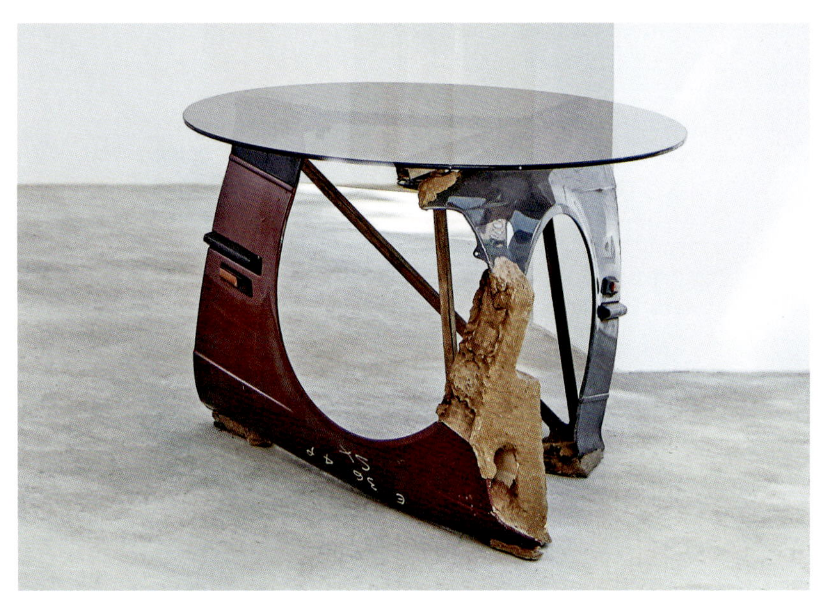

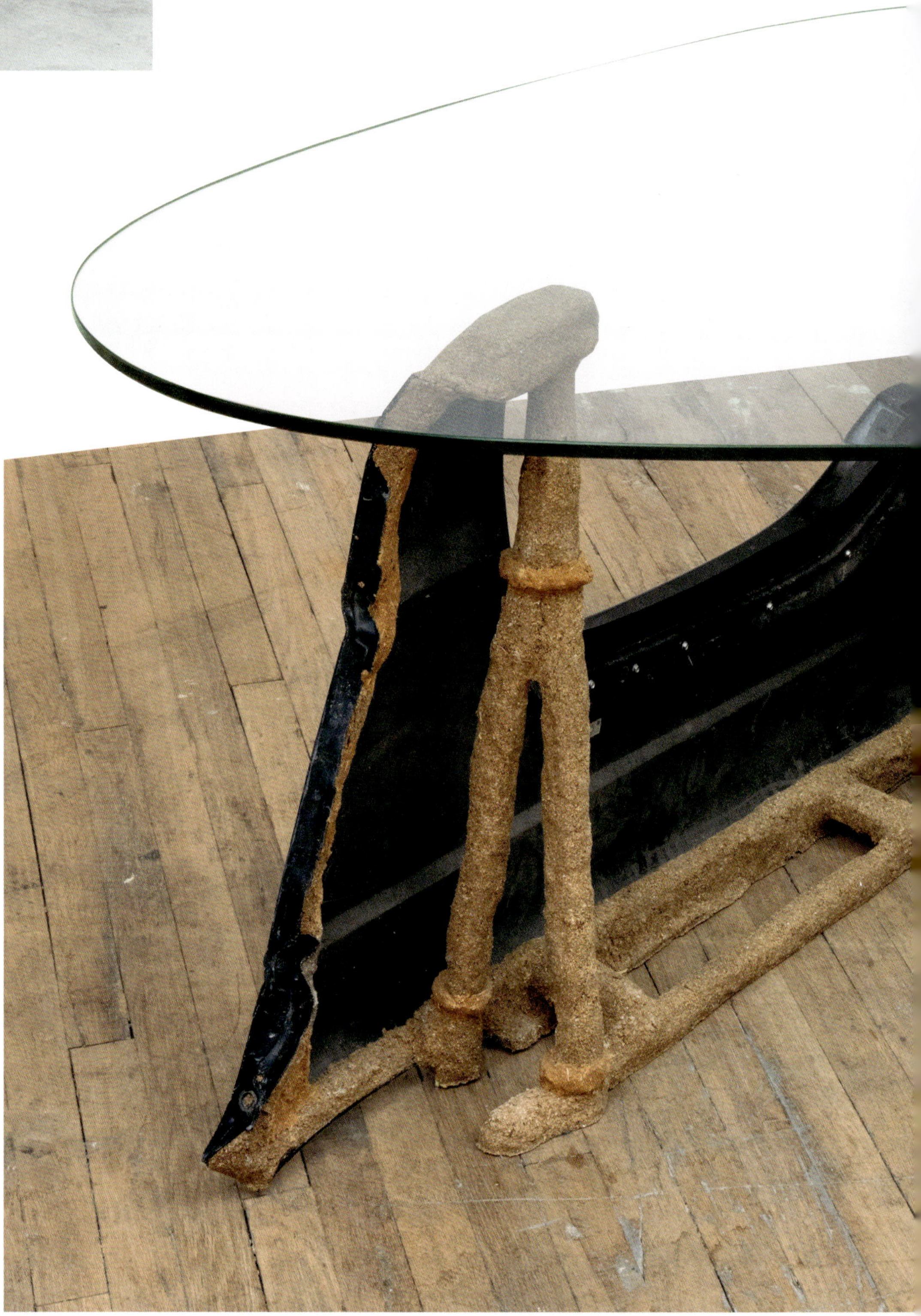

ABOVE
Jessi Reaves, Series 3 (Noguchi Fender Table), 2016
Car fenders, tempered glass, wood, sawdust, glue, hardware, and wood stain
29 1/8 × 59 × 41 3/8 inches (74 × 150 × 105 cm)

RIGHT
Jessi Reaves, Mind at the Rodeo (XJ Fender Table Noguchi Knockoff #2), 2016
Jeep Cherokee fenders (steel, plastic, auto paint) and glass tabletop
30 × 52 × 75 inches (76.2 × 132.1 × 190.5 cm)

Yes. Either way. Ultimately I would have stumbled back into painting. But that event was incredibly cathartic and very moving. When you are involved with a baby you are so open in a certain way. Emotionally you're crazy, but you are open because there is this little being around. And it is also very positive in terms of ego. It was the first time in my life that I really gave something to another human being. You have to or else they will die. It is very primitive, but then to really allow myself to be pulled away from my work gave me a new way of looking at it. It was very frustrating because my work was bad. That is when you really want to be doing it. But on the other hand, I just saw art and myself in a very different way. It kind of shattered my ego in relationship to my work.

The big thing that happened was that I realized it was something that I wanted to do for me. I needed just to do it. Even if I could only do it two hours a week. I wasn't doing it to get fame or recognition. The activity was very, very crucial to me. It was a very interesting thing to find out. A lot of people know that, but I didn't know it yet.

That was when?

That was in 1970 that I started to paint again.

What did the work look like when you started up these little paintings?

The first painting I did--and the work continued to be very similar to this for a year or so--was a kind of long, tall painting, a red painting with a sort of gray border around it. It looked like a baby's blanket. And inside the shape I kind of etched in these marks. I was thinking of a little house with a little moon rising above it. It had a kind of pattern sort of look but very, very flat. And primarily it was about the paint, about how the paint worked inside those little images. Most people never saw the images. Lots of times the people don't see the images in my work. I liked the painting. I immediately felt I was doing the right thing.

So it felt completely different?

It felt like it was mine. I was doing what I needed to do. I knew I could make it work. It was the sense that I was doing something I could resolve--if I stuck with it. And I don't think emotionally I feel any different from that now.

I understand what you are saying about that strongly felt connection to the work. Was there any other kind of external influence to it or did it just come from the inside?

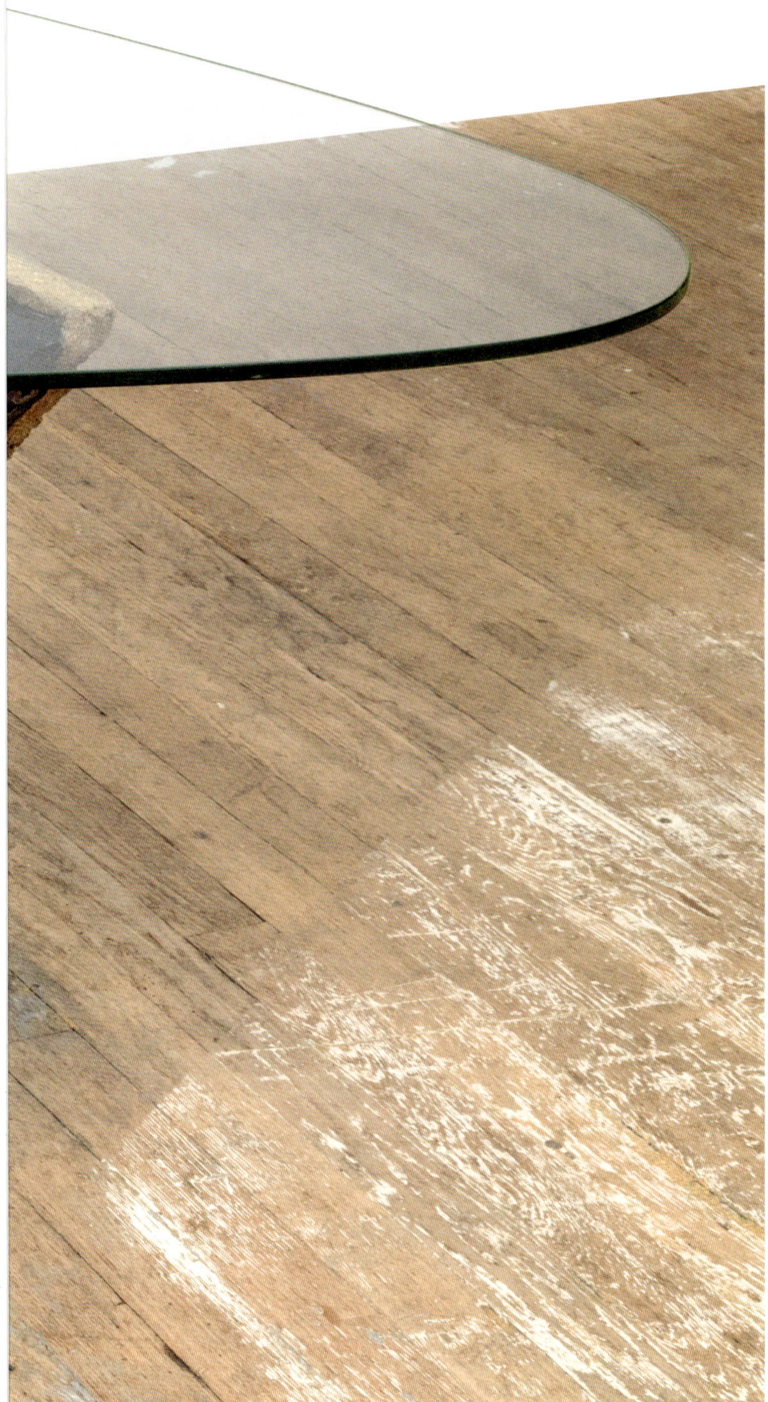

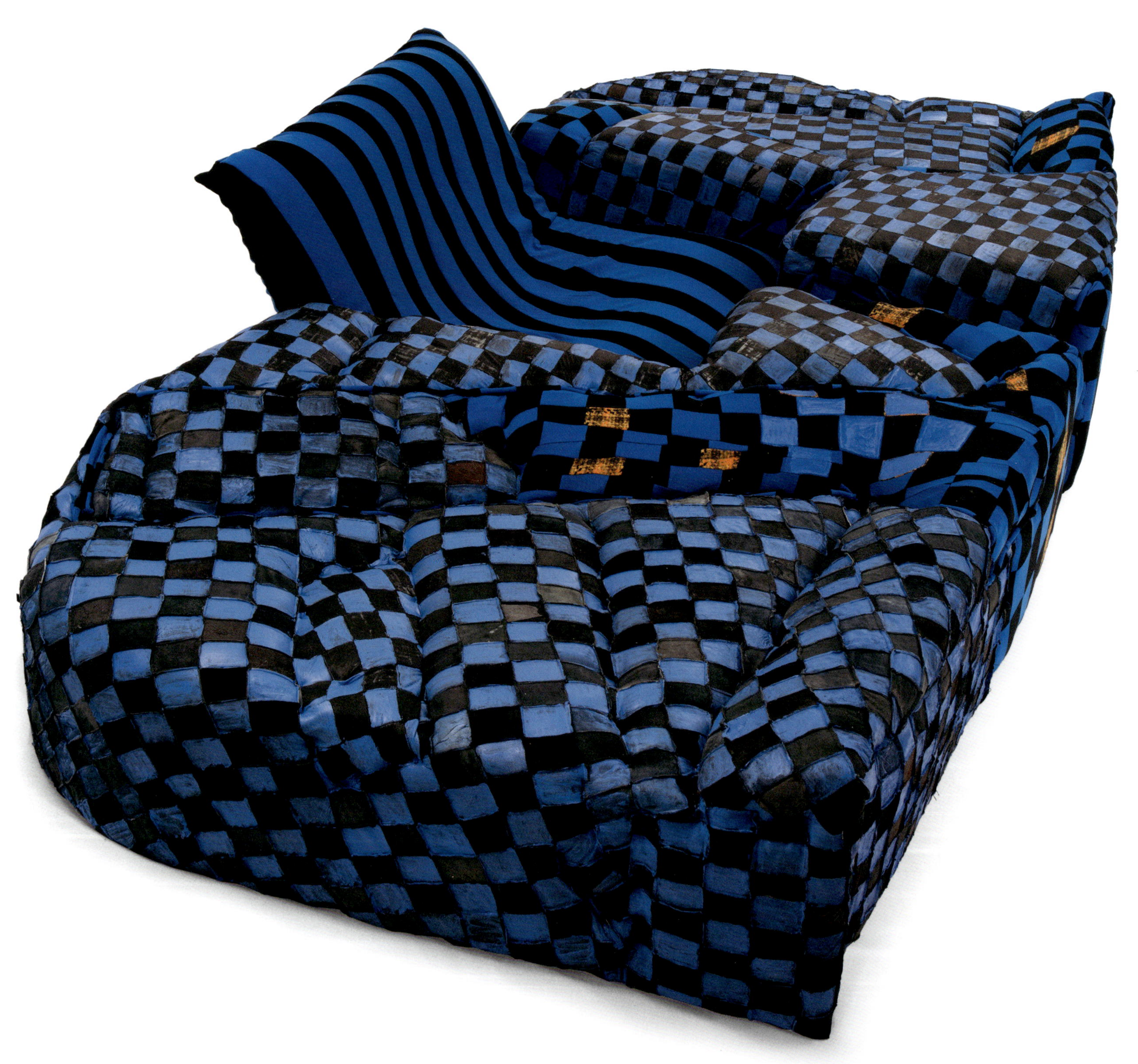

Jessi Reaves, Java Haunt Ottoman w/ Parked Chair, 2017
Plywood, foam, leather, fabric, paint, hardware, and webbing
30 × 62 × 120 inches (76.2 × 157.5 × 304.8 cm)

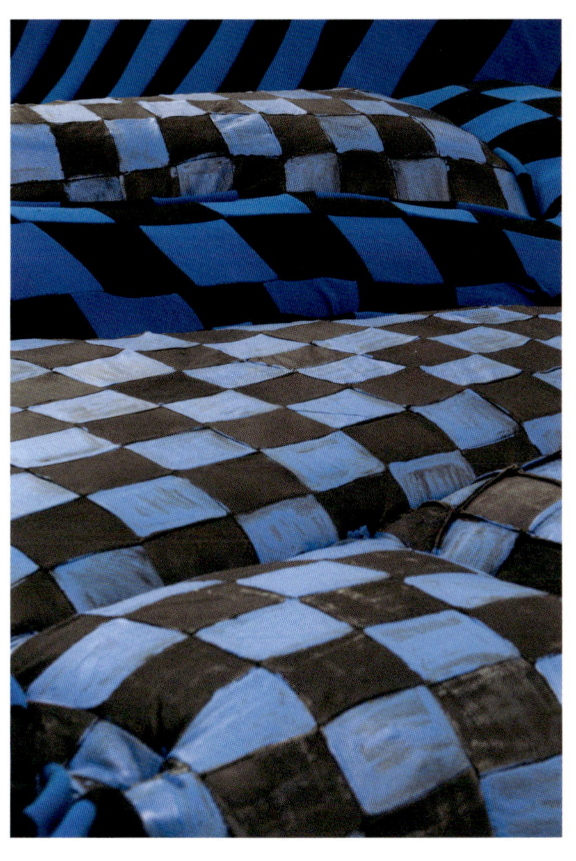

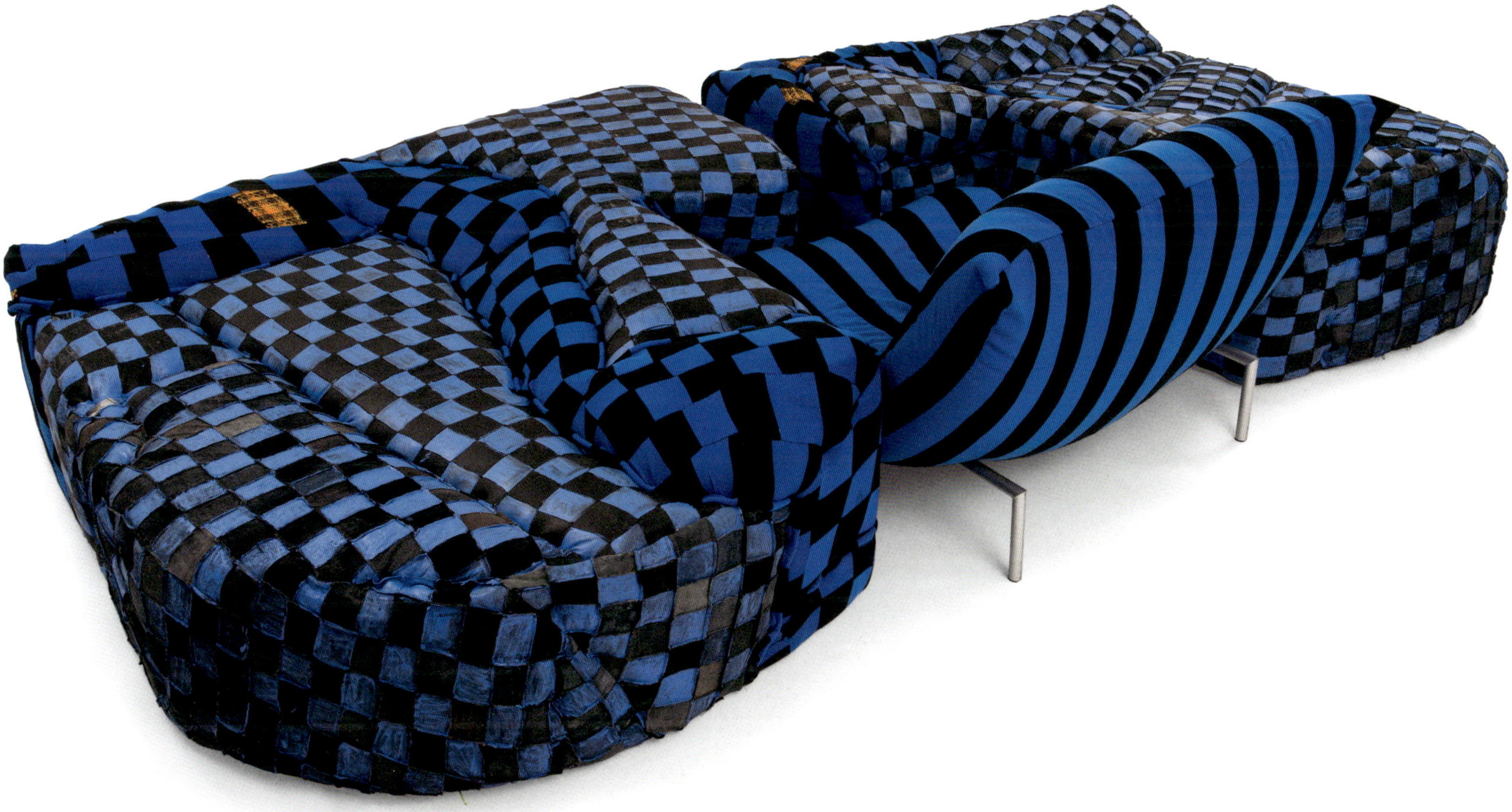

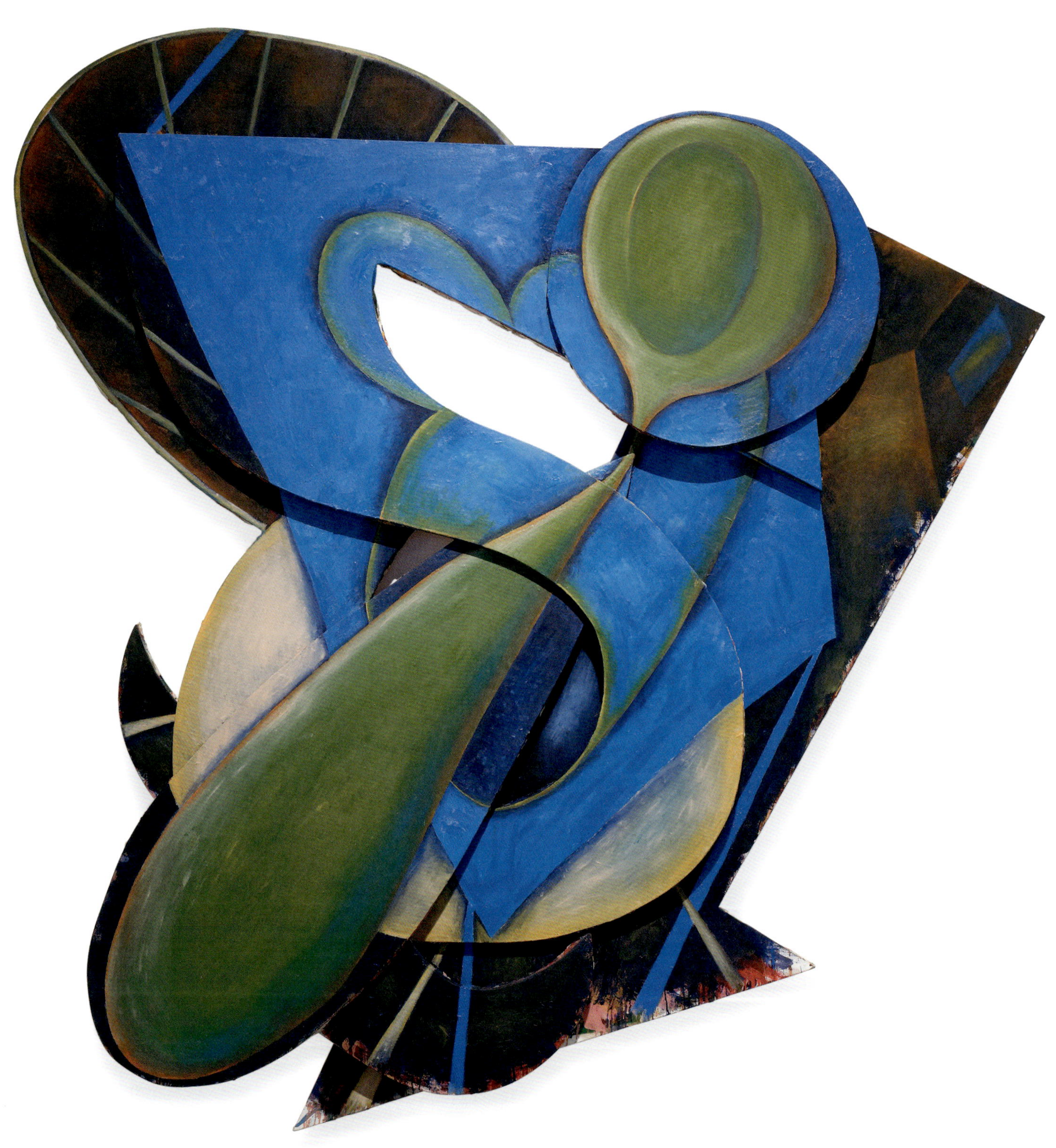

Elizabeth Murray, 1, 2, 3!, 1984
Oil on canvas
118 × 112 × 9 inches (299.7 × 284.5 × 22.9 cm)

OPPOSITE
Jessi Reaves, Rules Around Here (Waterproof Shelf), 2016
Plywood, vinyl, zippers, and marker
64 × 29 × 20 inches (162.6 × 73.7 × 50.8 cm)

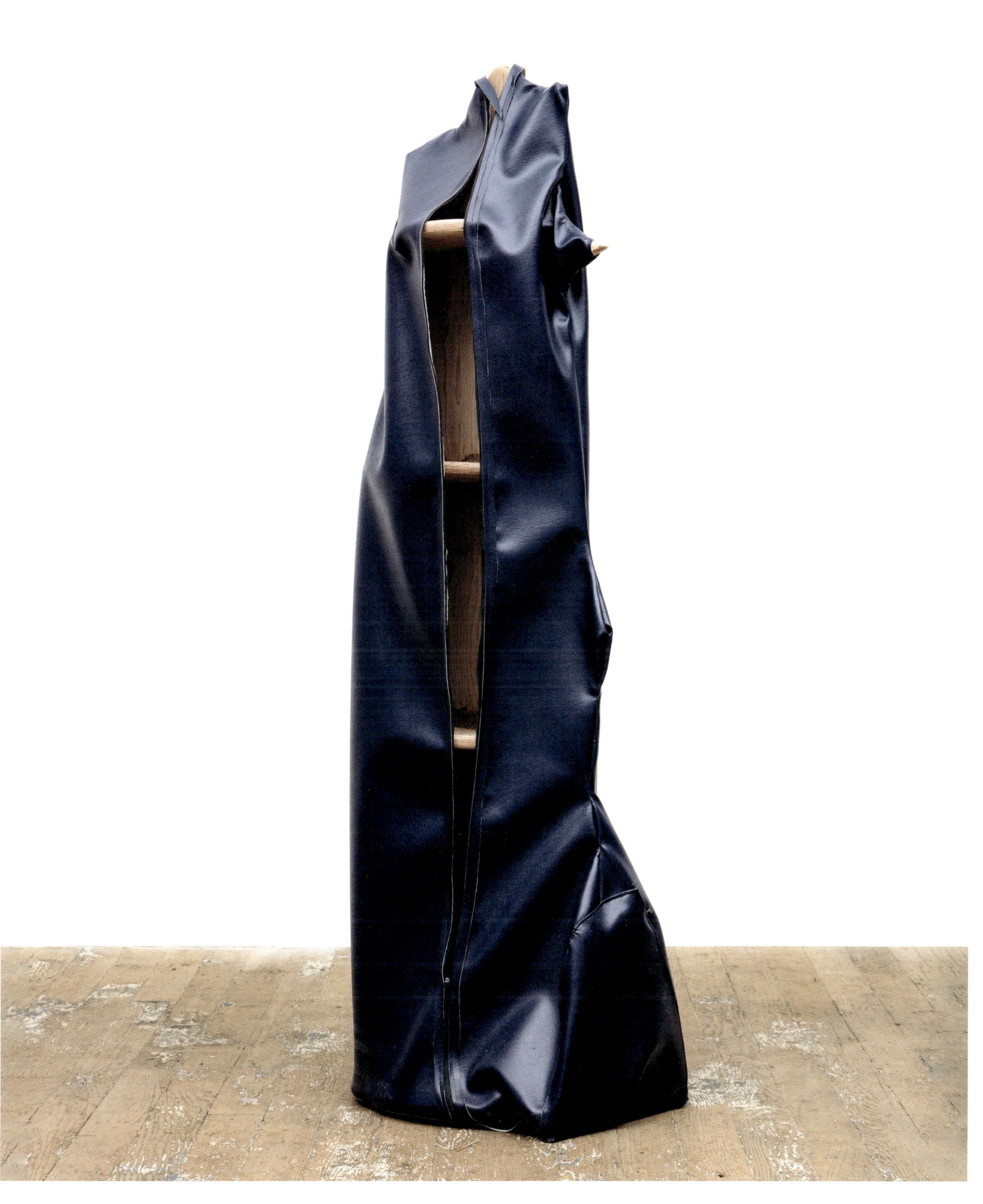

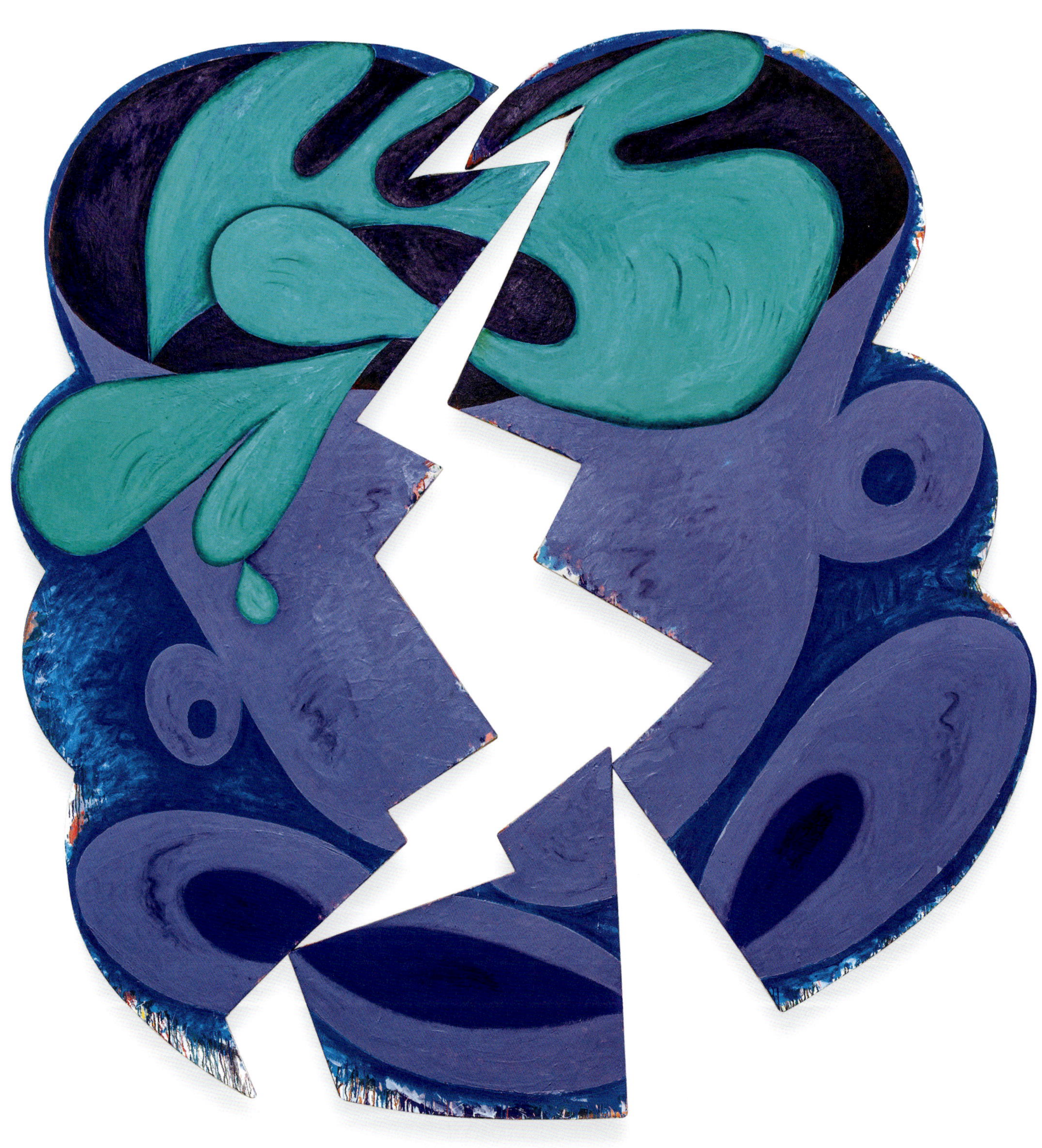

Elizabeth Murray, Wake Up, 1981
Oil on canvas
Three parts: 111 1/8 × 105 5/8 × 3 3/4 inches (282.3 × 268.3 × 9.5 cm) overall

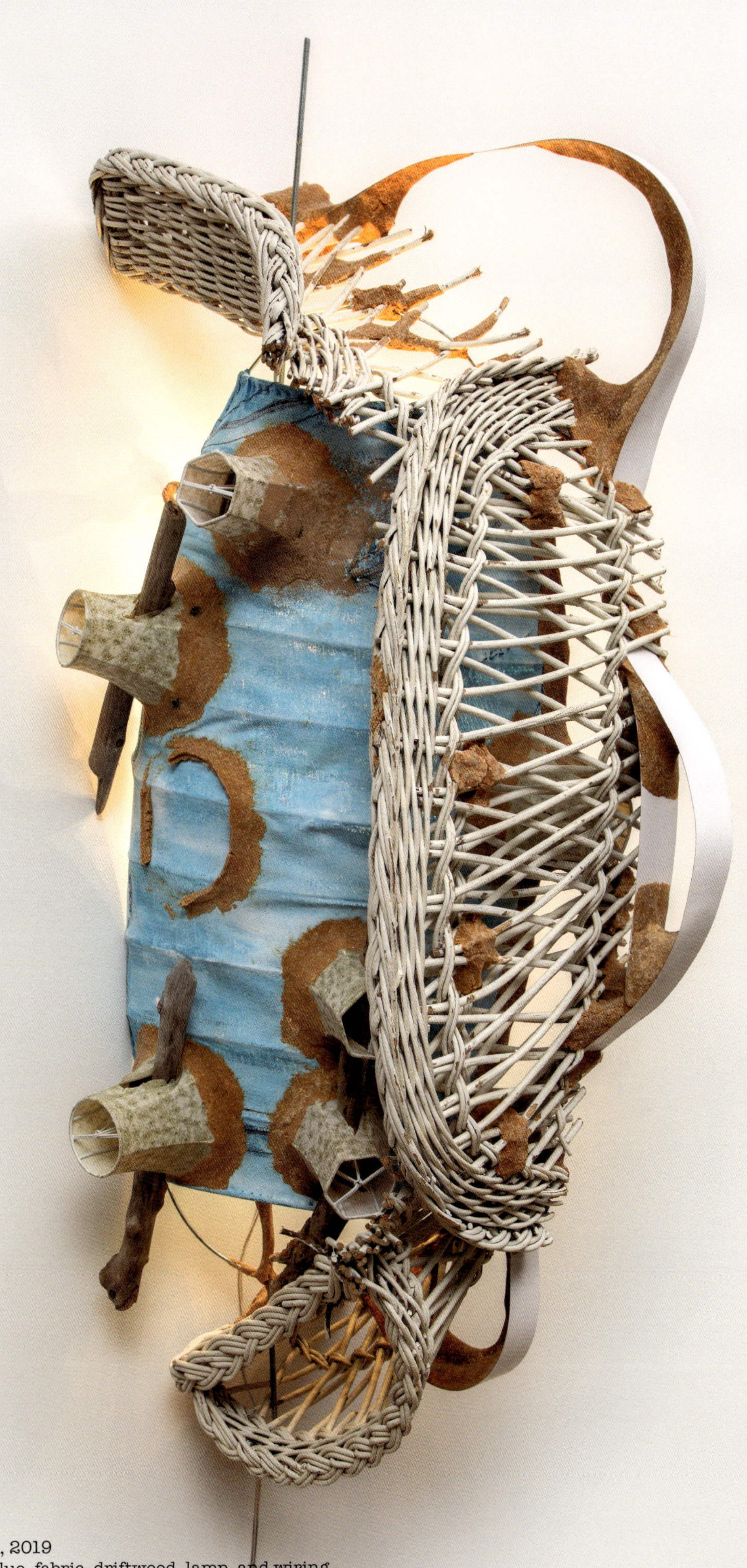

Jessi Reaves, Vicious circle wall lamp, 2019
Wicker, metal, paint, sawdust, wood glue, fabric, driftwood, lamp, and wiring
50 × 16 × 23 inches (127 × 40.6 × 58.4 cm)

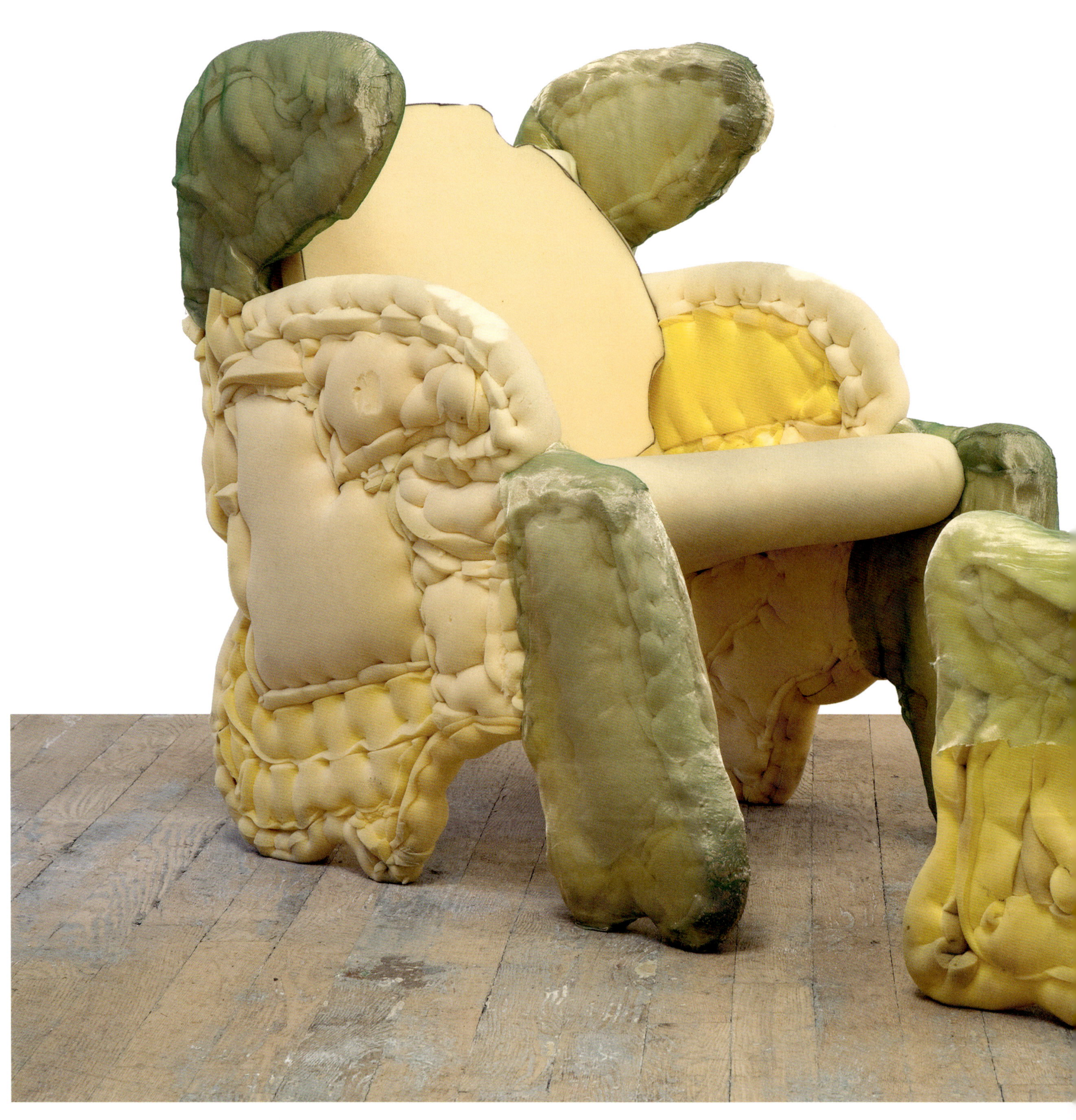

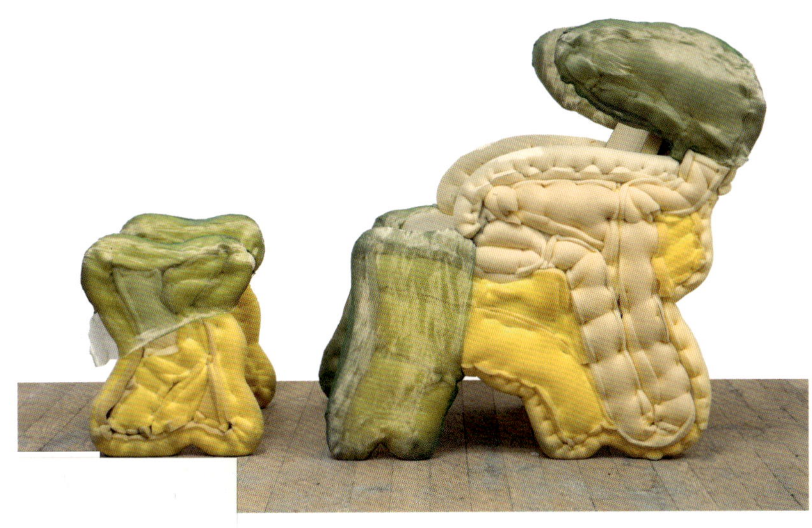

horrifi
images.
very mu
are ver
it's to
sexual.
I think
is in m
have th
you--wh
likes,
really

So peop
natura
your w
intent
you as

Yes. Bu
it is
if you
you th
thing,
place,
other
instea
consci
it is.
to me.
decisi
someth
or dum
feels
of the
me and
time.
with i

Given
with t
canvas
inside

For about a year it was pretty easy. And then that began to fall apart--I don't know how to say it--I guess I got bored with what I was doing. It's funny--for a while your limits are very exciting, then you get to the real limits of something you are doing. There is this wonderful moment when you get it. Then all of a sudden the limits, instead of being wonderful, these discoveries become clamps. Then you have to go forward or backtrack or whatever.

I did a couple years of these shapes, got more and more elaborate, more and more complex. I still wasn't sure why I was using the shapes, but I felt more and more interested in using shapes. The work, the paintings seemed to get more rigid, more tight. It became clear to me that the thing I needed to change was the paint inside. So basically for the last two years I have been involved in trying to soften the paint, to loosen it, to get less rigid with it, to develop different ways to think about what the paint can do.

It certainly isn't anything different than anybody else has done. But I feel more open now, I have loosened up. Primarily through working the shapes I have been able to do that. I began to get a clear feeling a couple years ago of what I wanted the shapes for. The shapes feel like catalysts; they become more like images. Which leaves me in a situation where I can do many different things on the inside of these edges. I can be very illusionistic and go totally against the outer edges, or I can play along with them. It throws up this kind of tension for me--a conflict that is quite interesting for me psychologically--the need to work out this conflict between inside and outside.

Can you talk a little about how you vary your paint surfaces, from flat to shiny and so on, and your reasons for manipulating them in those ways.

It is exciting. It is open-ended. I don't know what it will look like, it's very unpredictable. As unpredictable as things can be after you have driven a car down the same road for twenty years. You know a lot about what is going on--oil paint is oil paint. All of the changes in the surfaces, some people find them jarring and annoying actually, are something I really allow to happen. I mean I could make the surface perfectly flat or I could make it this way or that way, but the fact is that it does change unpredictably. This feels very exciting to me and very real. I like the roughness very, very much. I like the clumsiness of it--I have a tendency to really over-refine things--and this gives me something that goes against part of myself. I have a tendency to tighten, really screw things down. I always have to force myself to just let the paint happen.

Jessi Reaves, *Idol of the Hares*, 2014
Oak, polyurethane foam, silk, cotton, aluminum, and ink
38 × 28 × 48 inches (96.5 × 71.1 × 121.9 cm)

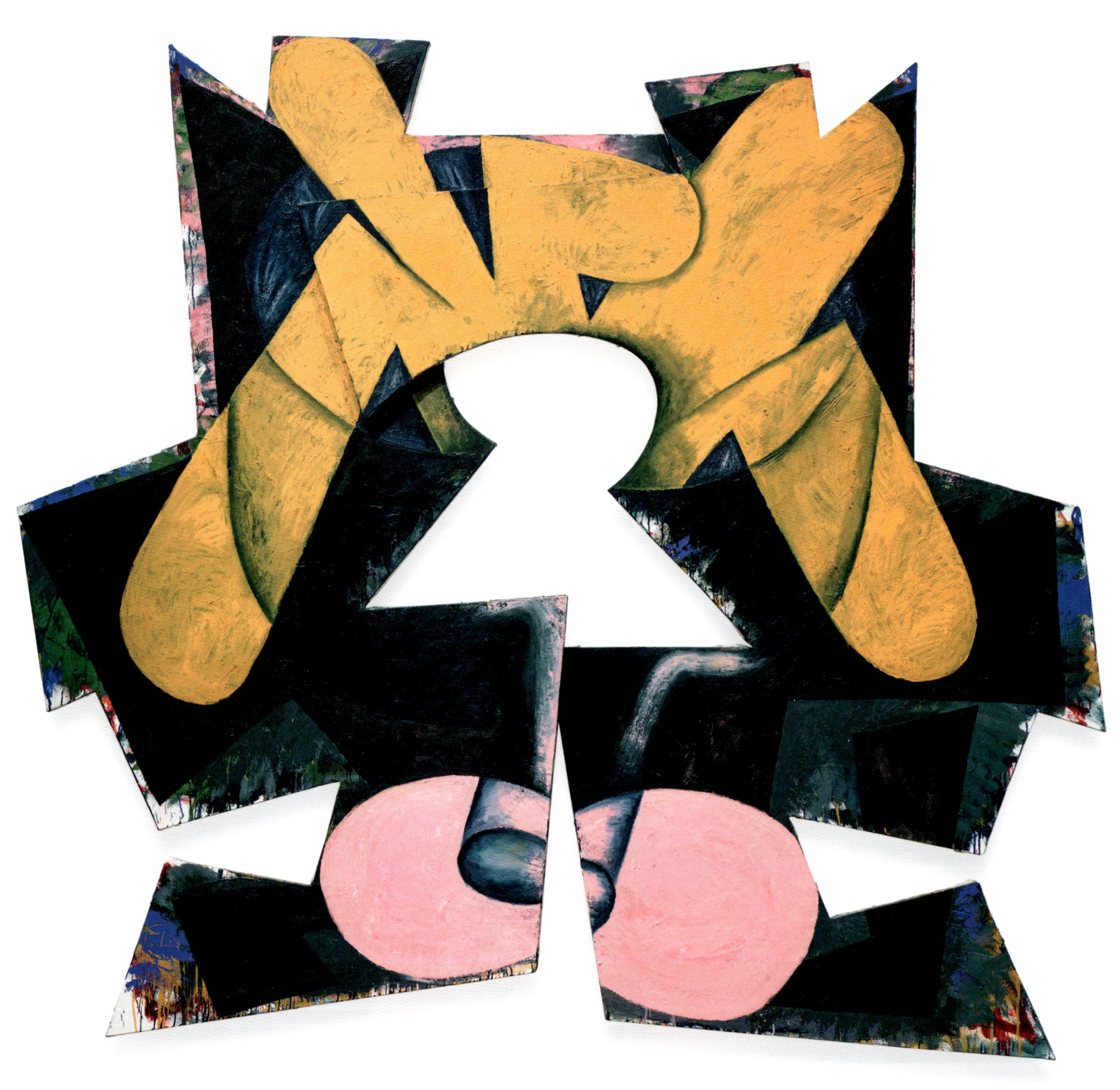

Elizabeth Murray, Keyhole, 1982
Oil on canvas
99 7/16 × 110 1/2 inches (252.6 × 280.6 cm)

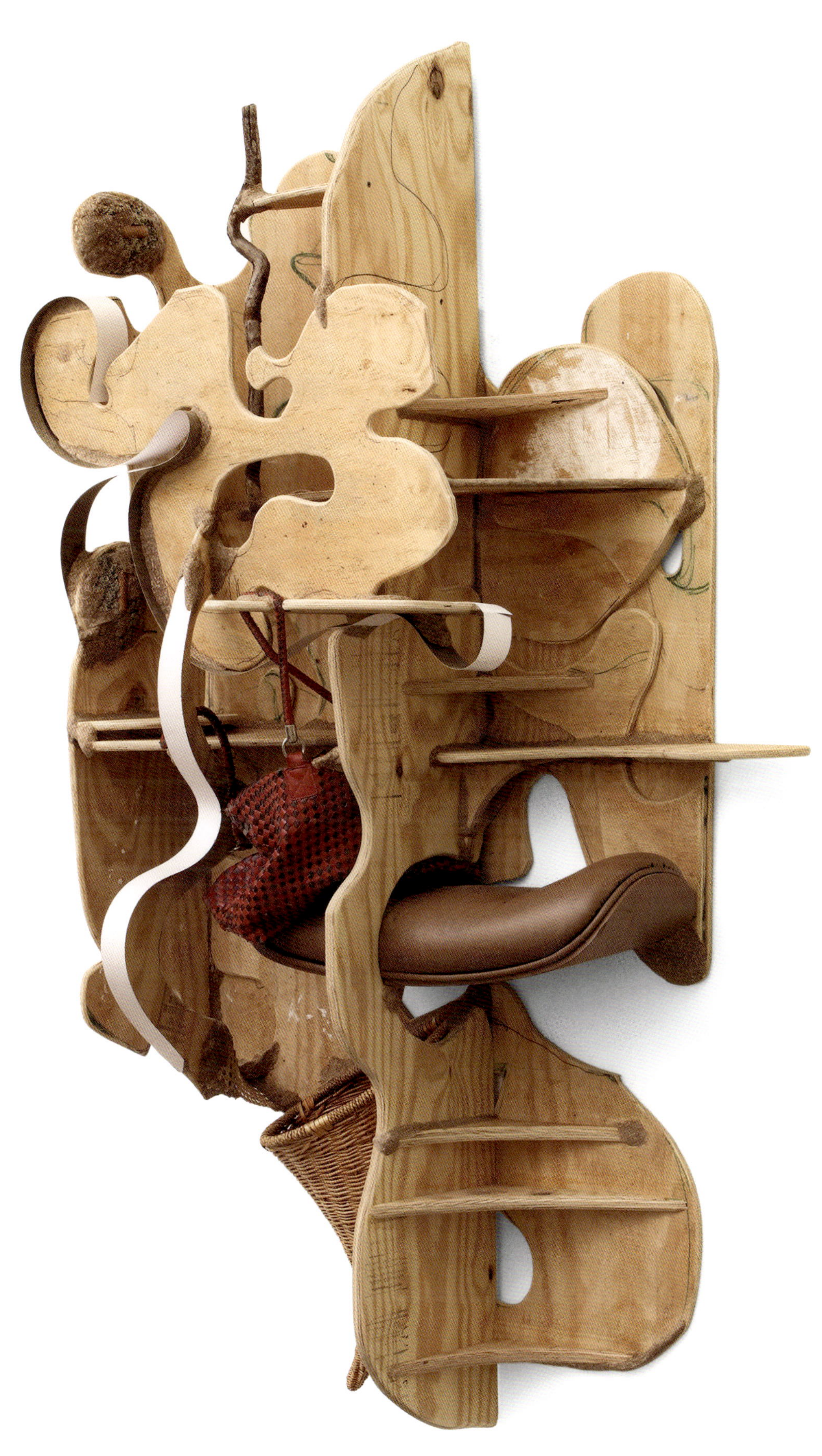

Jessi Reaves, Walking and looking for you, 2017
Plywood, wood, found objects, sawdust, wood glue, ink, laminate, and paint
75 × 35 × 18 inches (185.4 × 88.9 × 45.7 cm)

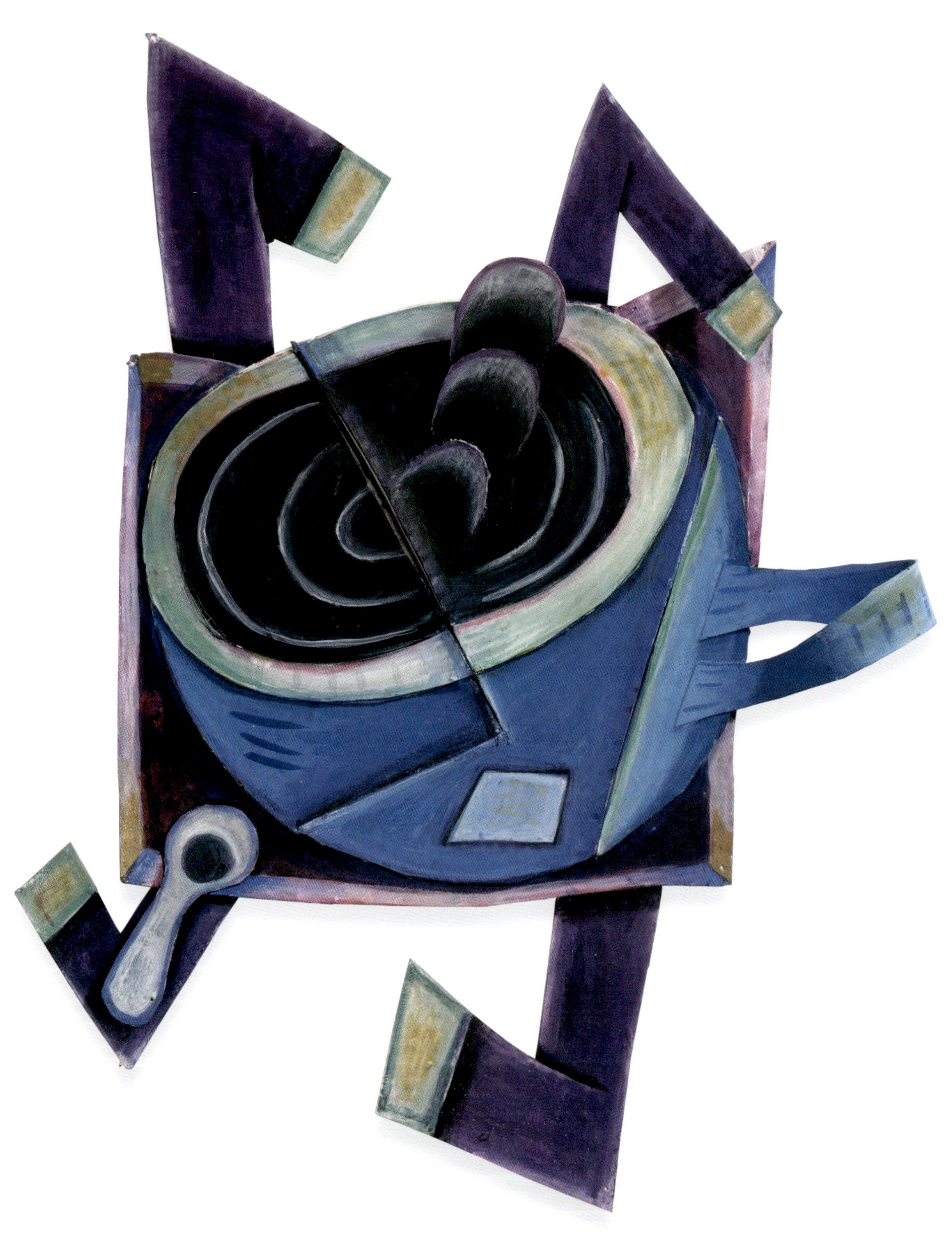

Elizabeth Murray, Puff, 2000
Gouache on paper
13 × 11 inches (33 × 28 cm)
60

OPPOSITE, 63
Jessi Reaves, Bitches Bonnet Seat, 2016
Plywood, wood, foam, nylon, embroidery, cotton, and leather
33 × 27 × 37 inches (83.8 × 68.6 × 94 cm)

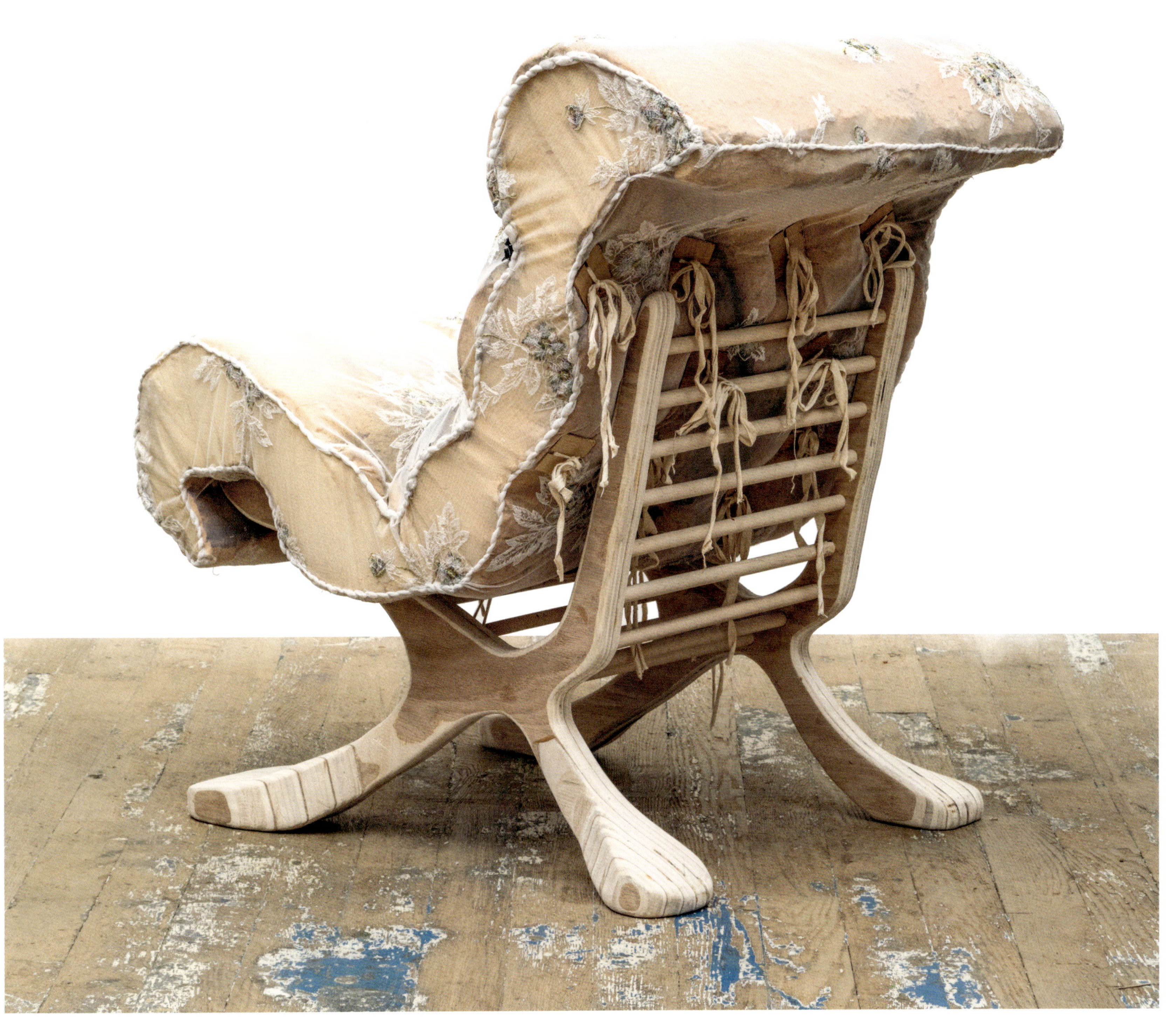

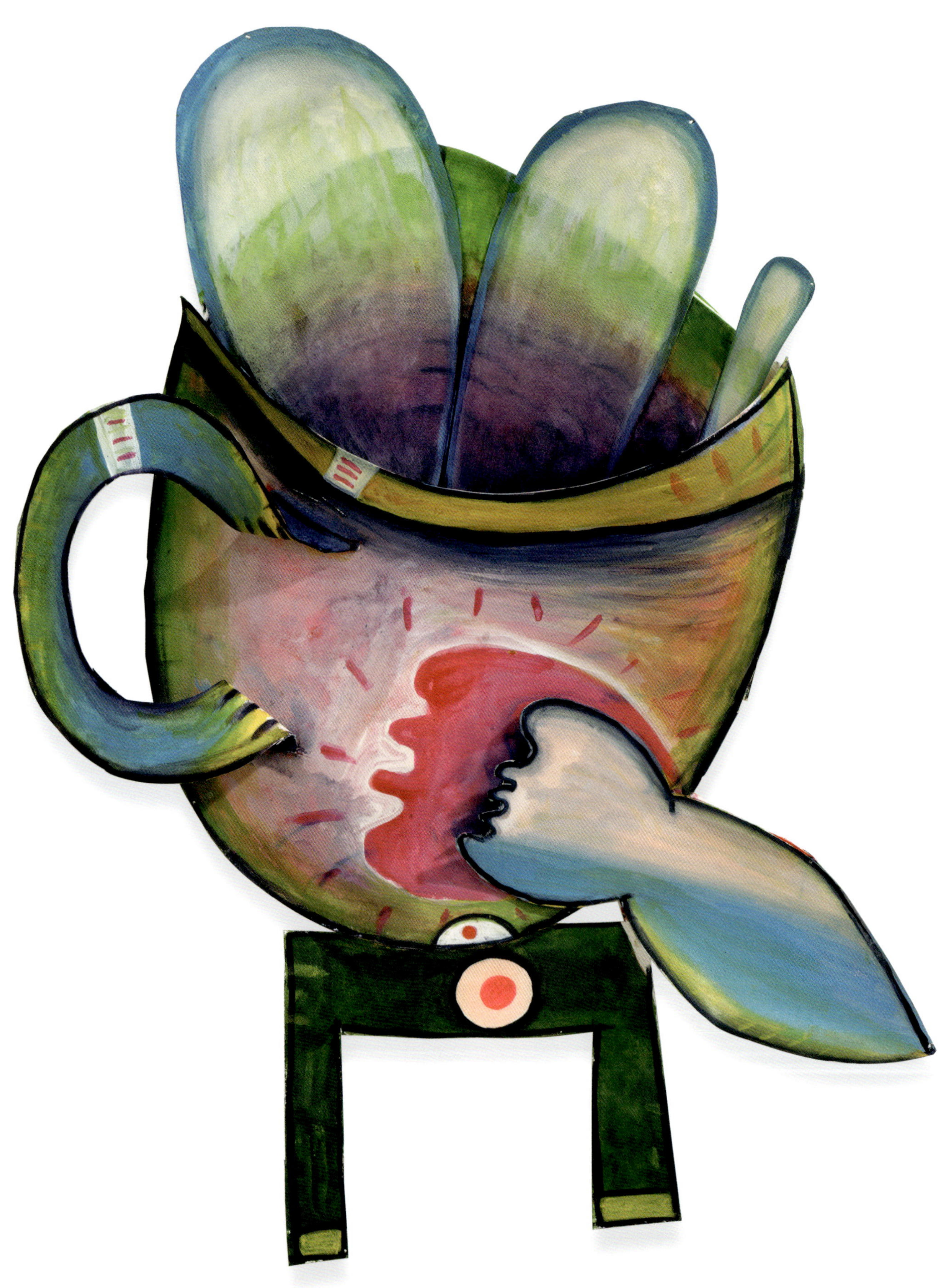

Elizabeth Murray, Wild Chase Brush, 2001
Gouache on paper
18 1/4 × 14 inches (46.4 × 35.6 cm)
62

64, 65
Jessi Reaves, NY state cabinet, 2019
Wood, plexiglass, paint, sawdust, wood glue, and hardware
97 × 42 × 32 inches (246.4 × 106.7 × 81.3 cm)

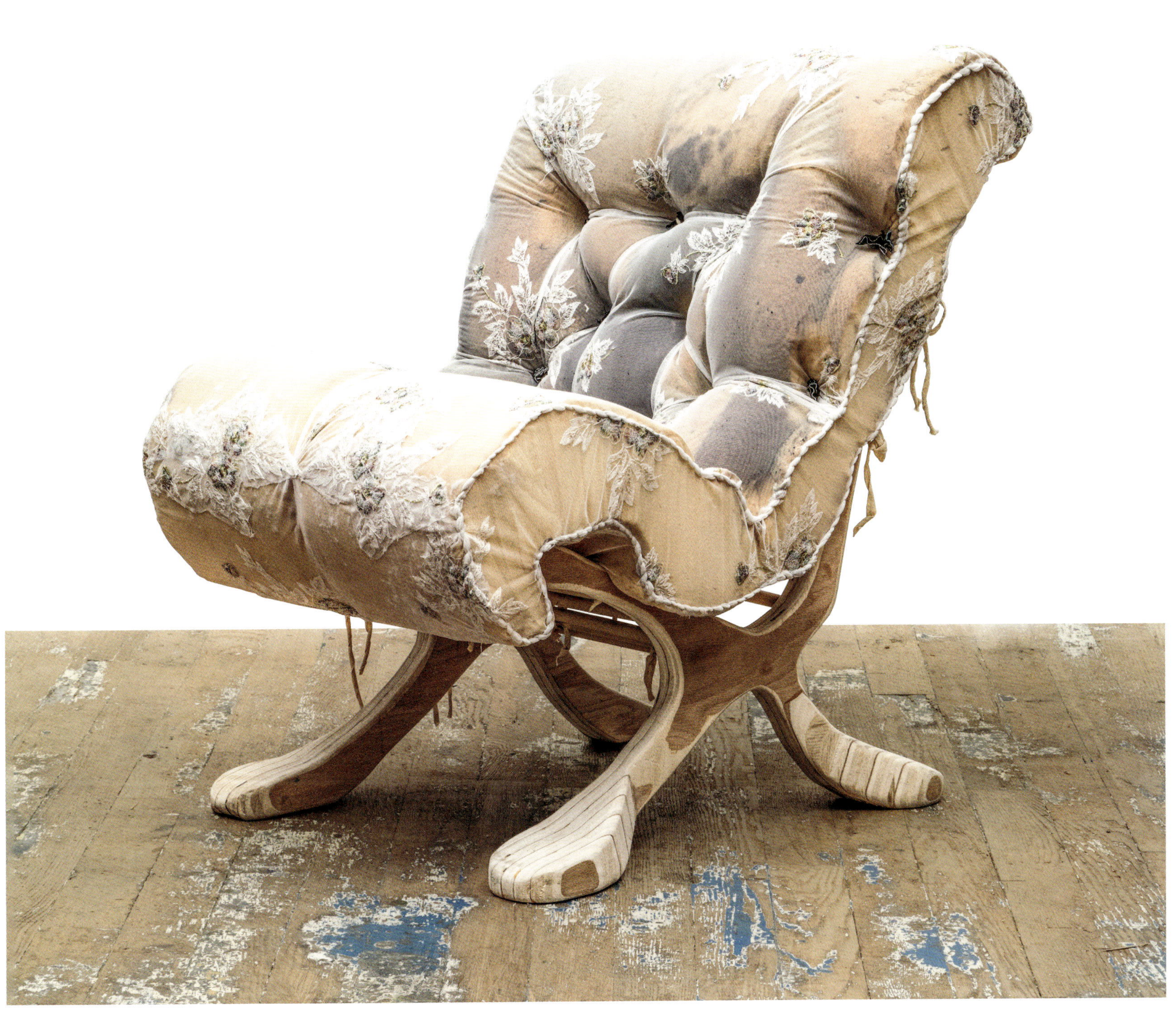

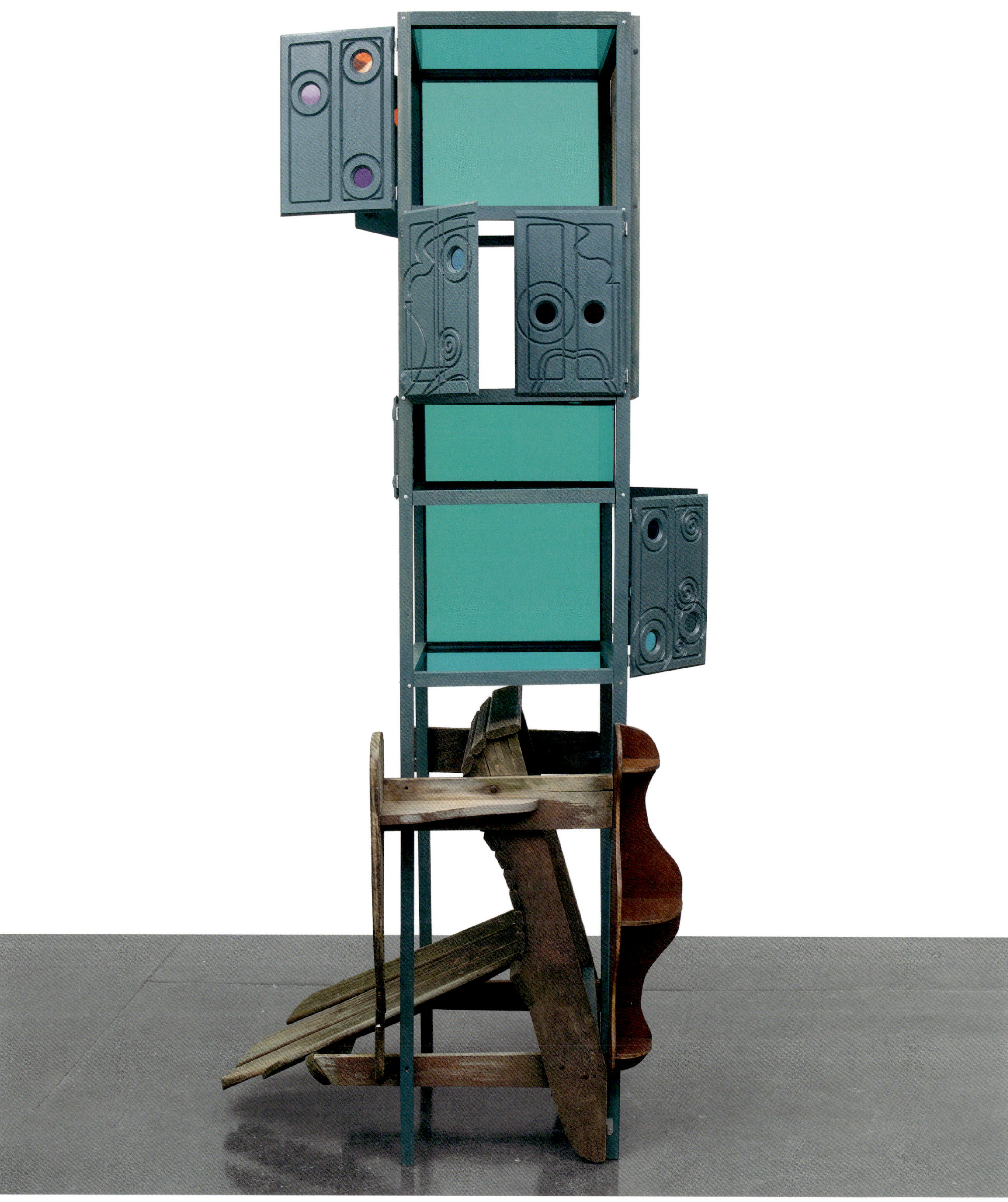

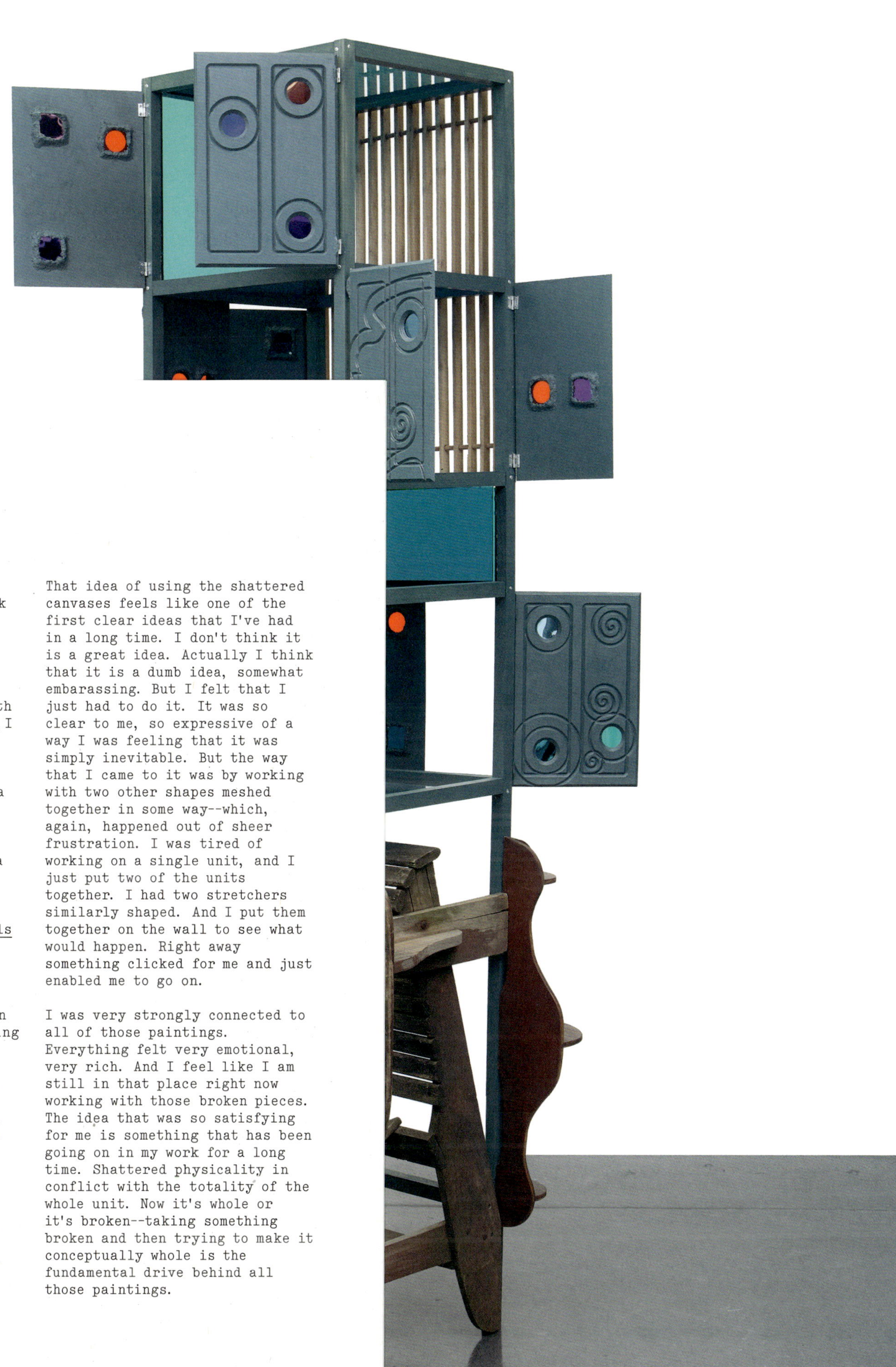

Usually I start intuitively--I just start to paint. I just work on the canvas. Sometimes I do some drawings. I have a little book, record book, and I do little drawings inside that but they are nothing. I just throw them away, or whatever. Just with a ballpoint pen. Recently since I have had more time and energy I've been doing more drawing around the painting or for the painting. I certainly don't do a drawing before and then do the painting. That I've never done. It would kill it for me. I don't think that way. It wouldn't be a suitable way for me to work.

So there is something about the life of the process which appeals to you.

Yes. It's what I do. If I analyzed it before that I would really have nothing to do. I can virtually not imagine approaching the work that way because it is so intensely about this relationship, this time that is new and very unknown when you begin, and then gets more known and then gets unknown. It would take the life out of it completely for me to work any other way.

In the show that you had in May [1981], you began exploding the entire canvas into small canvas fragments that all fit together into a whole. Would you talk a little about the ideas that led up to that work?

That idea of using the shattered canvases feels like one of the first clear ideas that I've had in a long time. I don't think it is a great idea. Actually I think that it is a dumb idea, somewhat embarassing. But I felt that I just had to do it. It was so clear to me, so expressive of a way I was feeling that it was simply inevitable. But the way that I came to it was by working with two other shapes meshed together in some way--which, again, happened out of sheer frustration. I was tired of working on a single unit, and I just put two of the units together. I had two stretchers similarly shaped. And I put them together on the wall to see what would happen. Right away something clicked for me and just enabled me to go on.

I was very strongly connected to all of those paintings. Everything felt very emotional, very rich. And I feel like I am still in that place right now working with those broken pieces. The idea that was so satisfying for me is something that has been going on in my work for a long time. Shattered physicality in conflict with the totality of the whole unit. Now it's whole or it's broken--taking something broken and then trying to make it conceptually whole is the fundamental drive behind all those paintings.

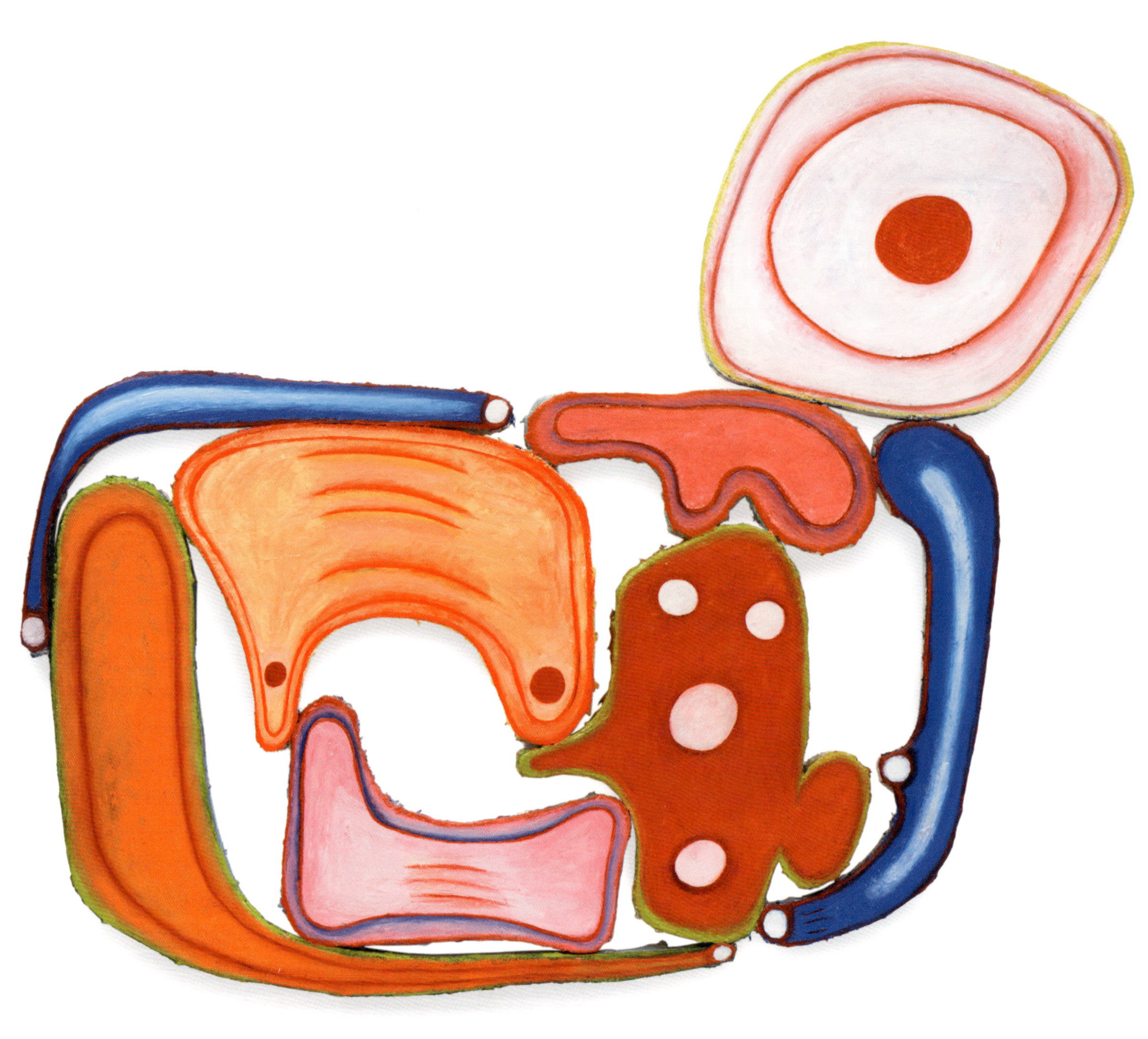

Elizabeth Murray, Bare, 1999–2000
Oil on canvas
36 1/2 × 43 1/2 inches (92.7 × 110.5 cm)

OPPOSITE
Jessi Reaves, Cesca Leaves the Stack (Modified Chair), 2016
Polyurethane foam, chrome-plated tubular steel frame, hardwood beech with cane inserts, rayon, nylon, plastic, ink, and hardware
48 × 18 1/2 × 28 inches (121.9 × 47 × 71.1 cm)

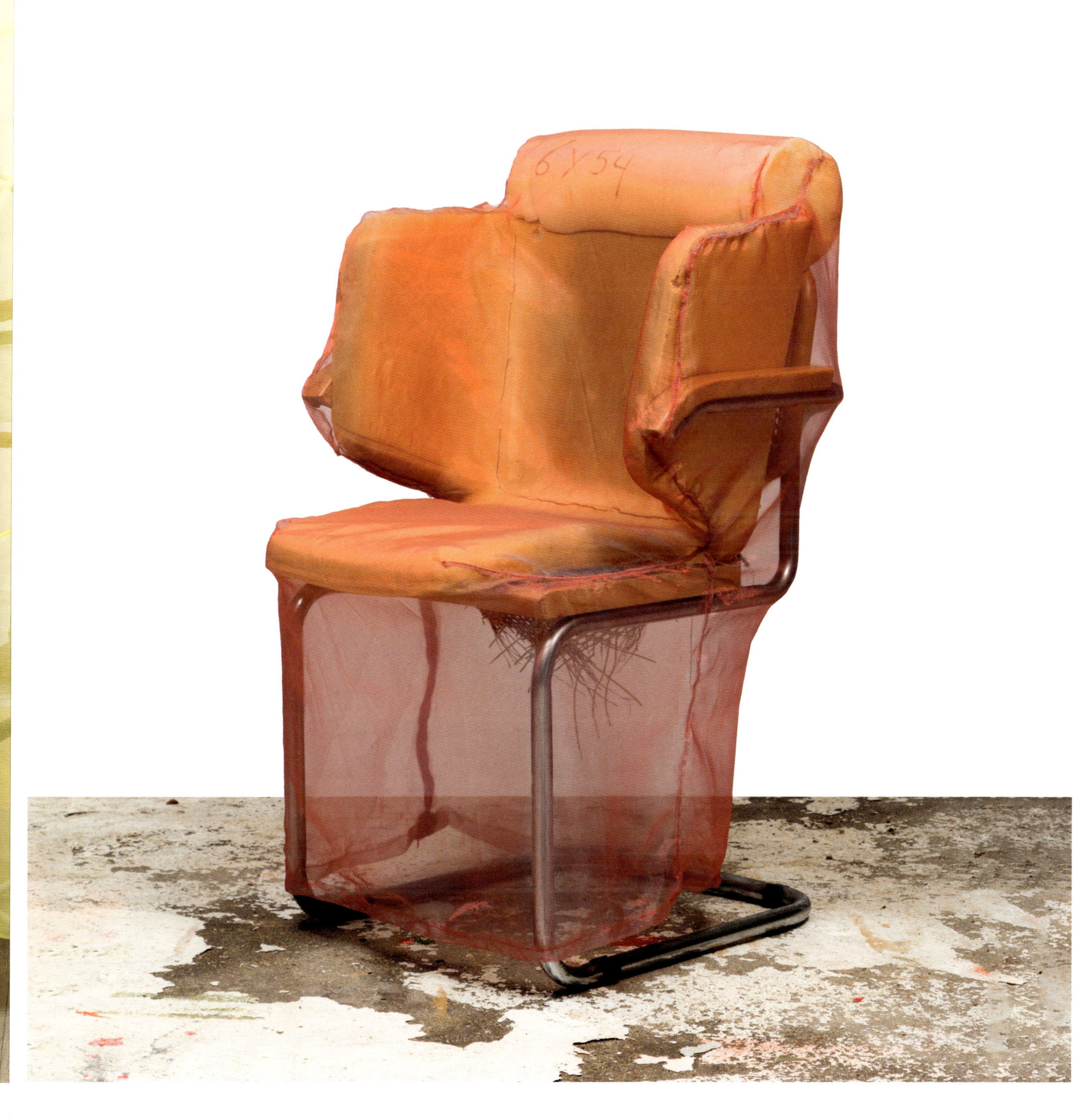
6X54

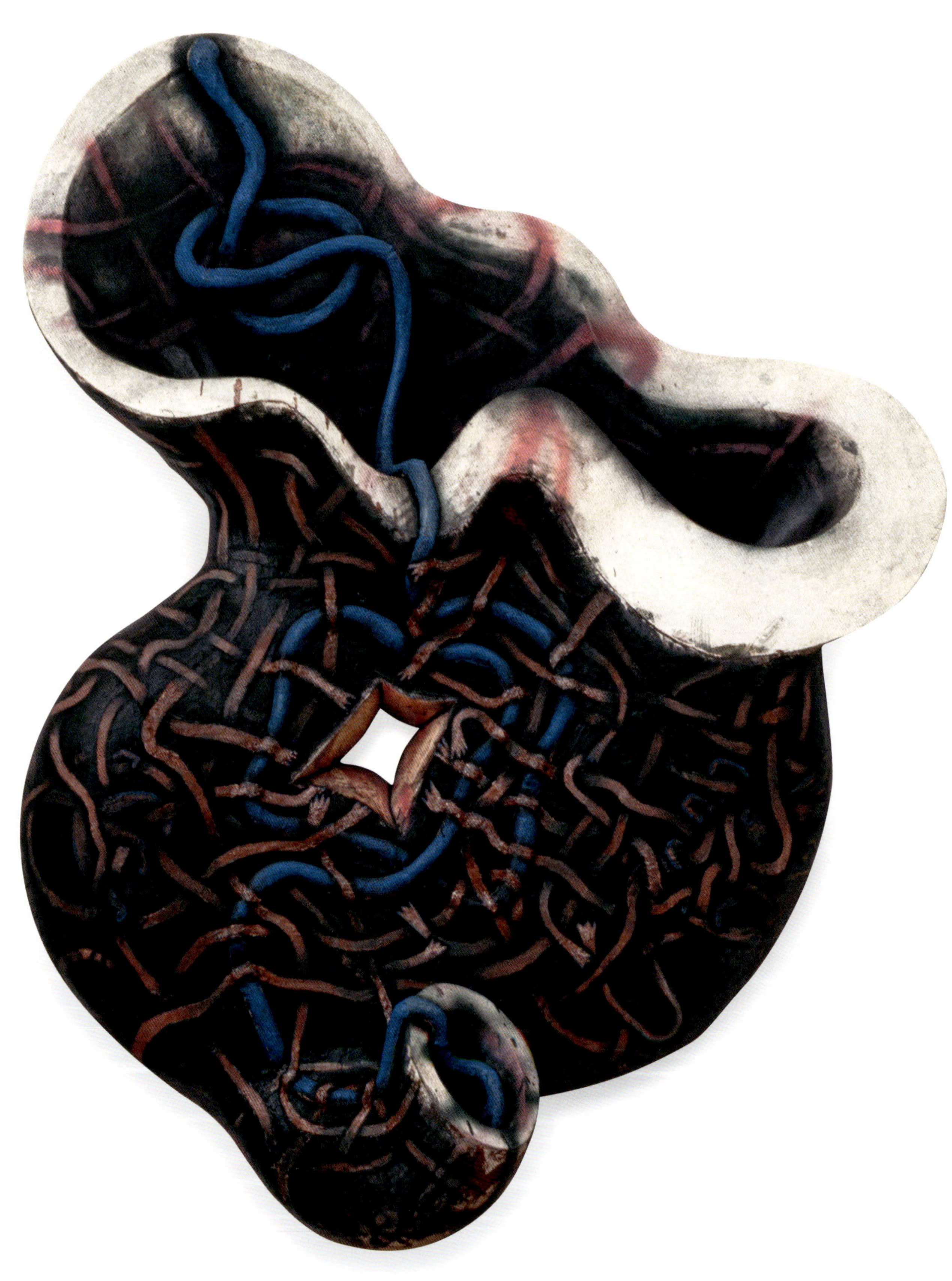

Elizabeth Murray, Tangled, 1989–90
Oil on canvas on wood
83 1/2 × 66 × 19 inches (212.1 × 167.6 × 48.3 cm)

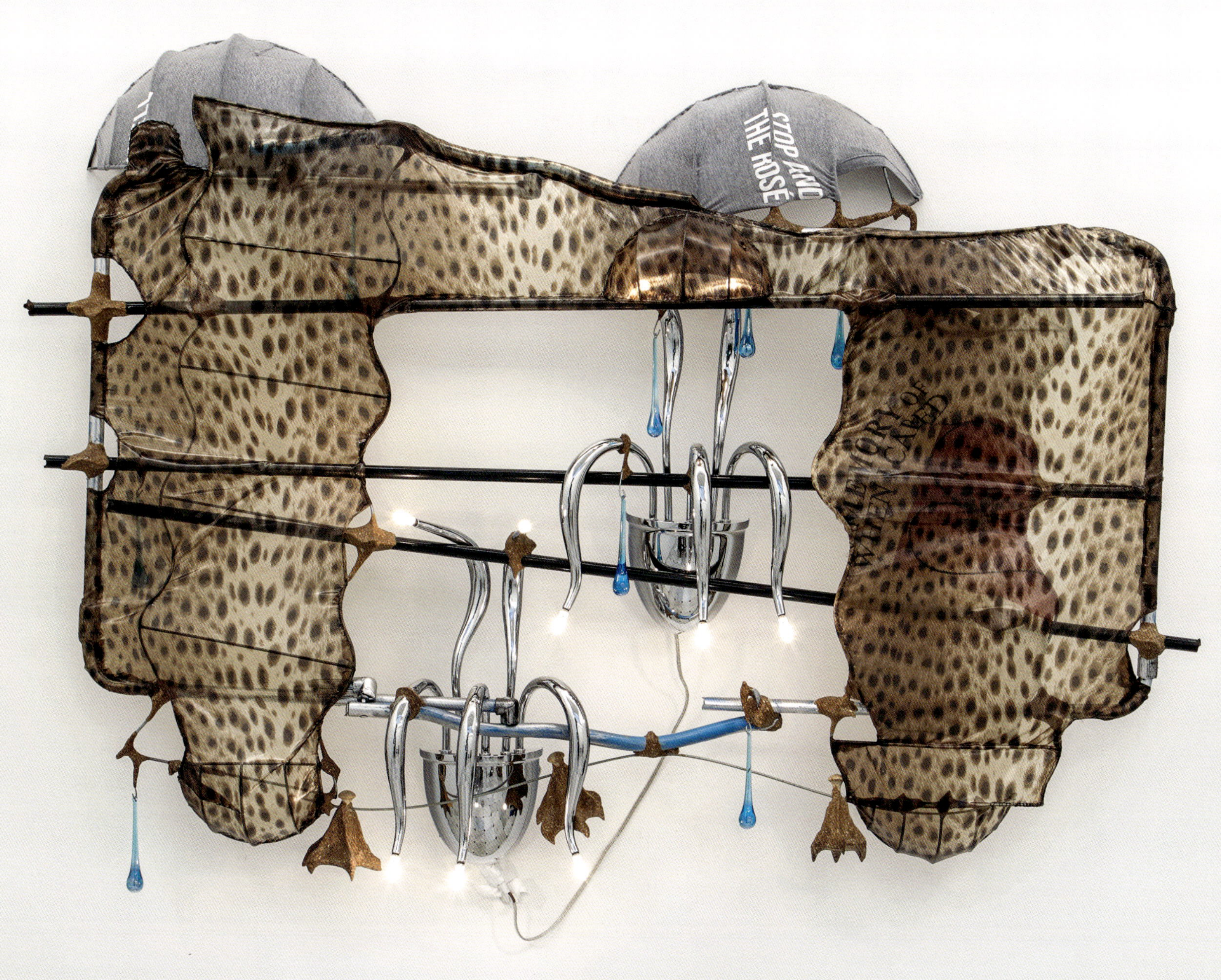

Jessi Reaves, Mantelpiece Sconce, 2019
Metal, glass, fabric, sawdust, wood glue, lamp wiring, and bulbs
41 × 58 × 12 inches (104.1 × 147.3 × 30.5 cm)

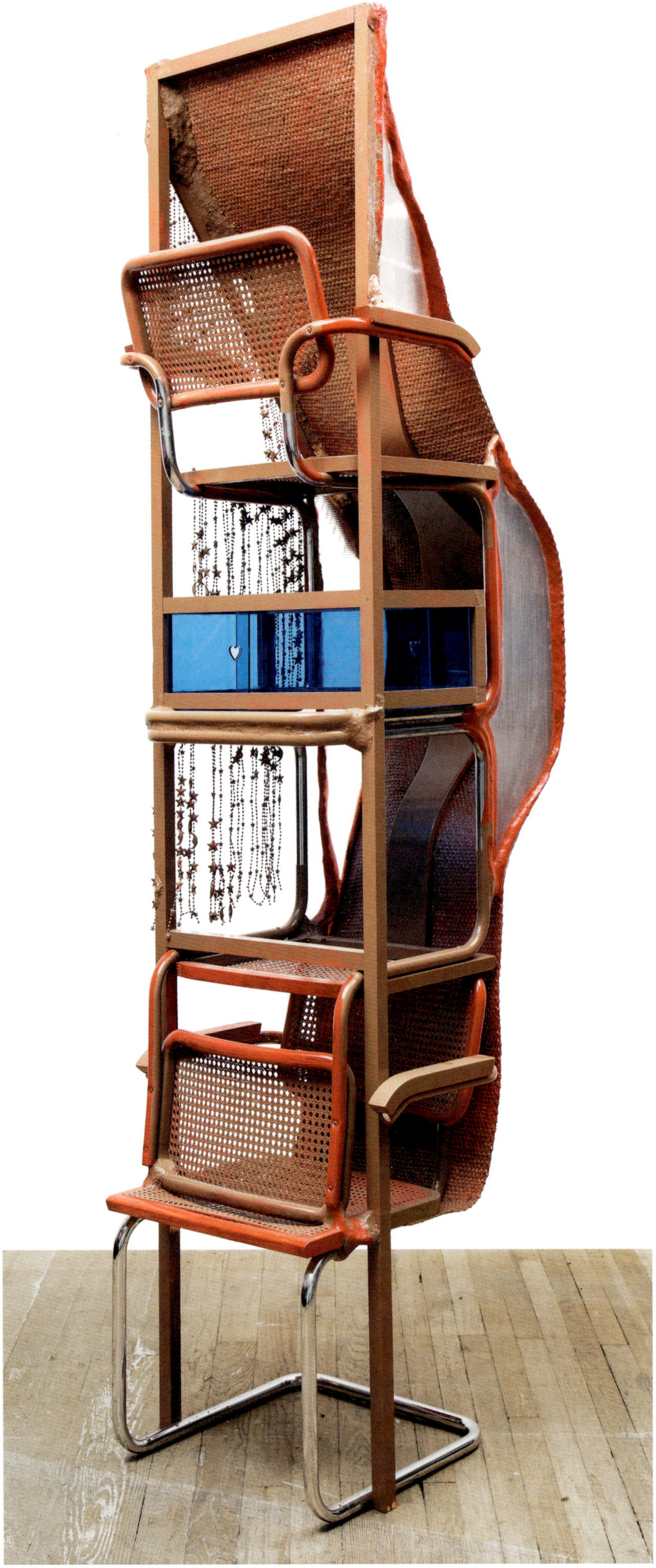

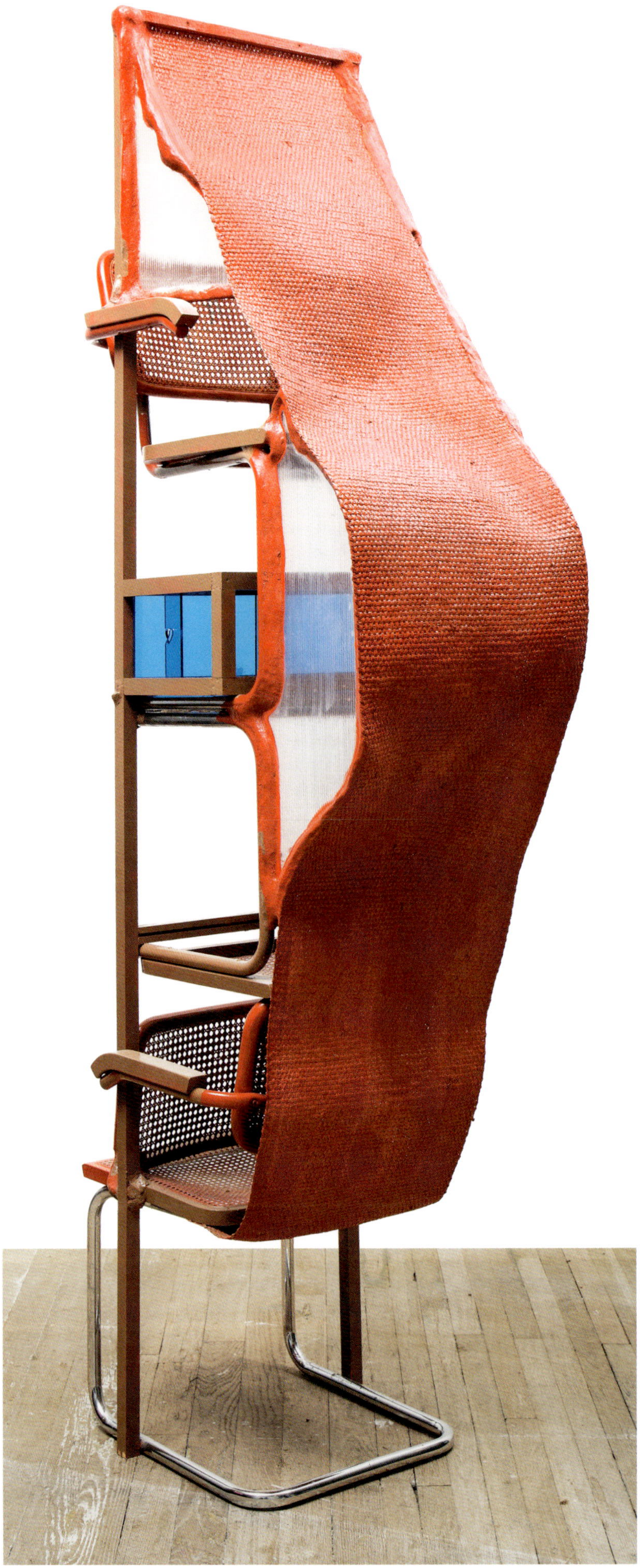

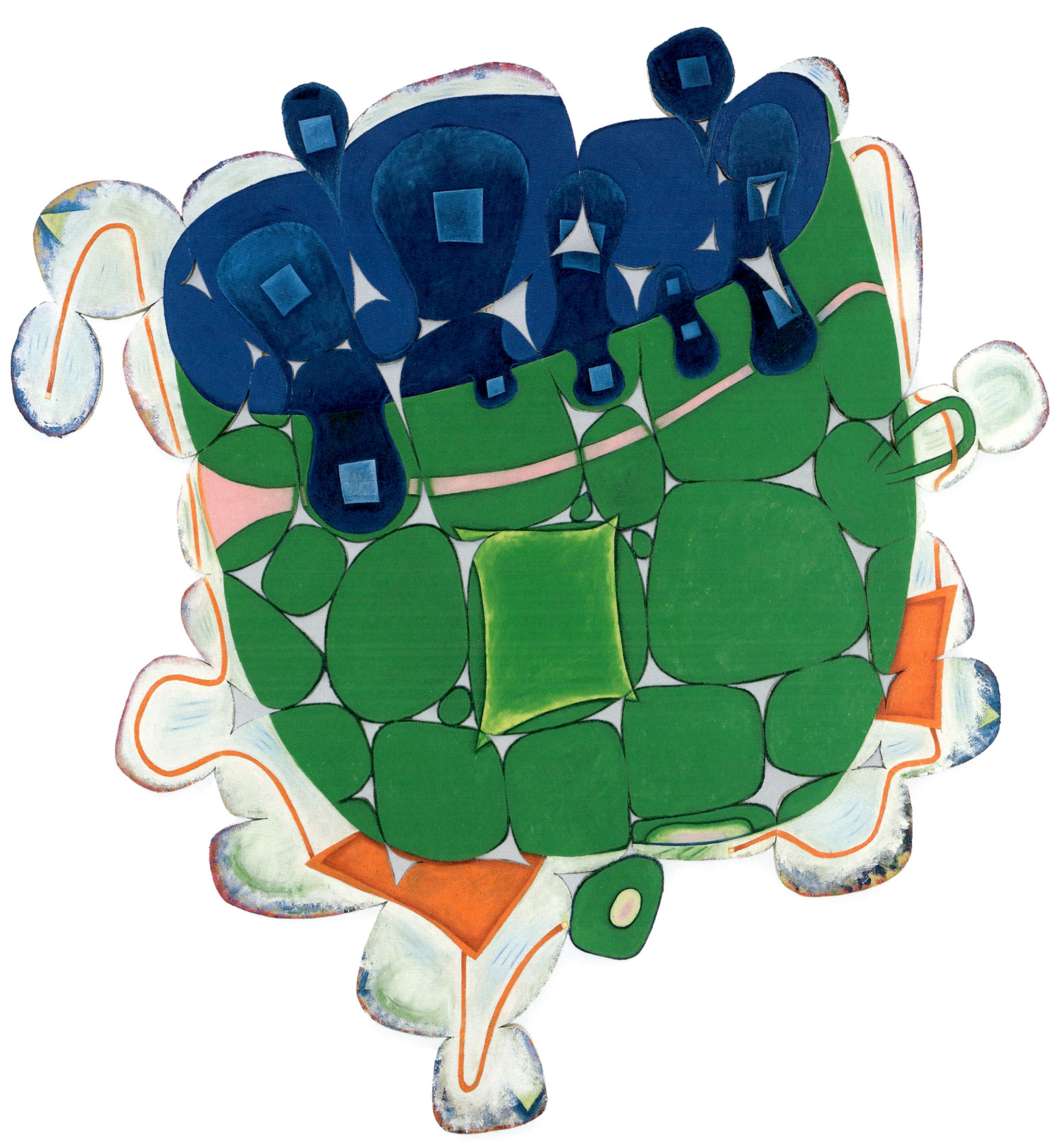

OPPOSITE
Jessi Reaves, Blue heart shelf, 2019
Wood and metal chairs, woven fabric, plexiglass, paint, plastic, sawdust, and wood glue
96 × 23 × 30 inches (243.8 × 58.4 × 76.2 cm)

ABOVE
Elizabeth Murray, Cry Baby, 2000
Oil on canvas
105 1/4 × 105 3/4 inches (267.3 × 268.6 cm)

With great pleasure, Contemporary Arts Museum Houston (CAMH) presents Wild Life: Elizabeth Murray & Jessi Reaves. This exhibition, curated by Rebecca Matalon and organized by CAMH, spans five decades of production by two fearless artists. As a noncollecting museum, CAMH has the rare latitude and charge to aggressively look forward, even as we reanimate historic arcs of contemporary art. This exhibition lands at a critical moment for CAMH, and for society: as we look to the end of a global pandemic, Wild Life reminds us that what falls apart may yet be created anew.

With this exhibition and book, Matalon recognizes a link between artists who share a particular and deep investment in upending formal tropes of "good taste" through remarkable shifts toward bodily and domestic visual narratives. Their works—which range from painting, assemblage, sculpture, and delirious hybrids of these media—explode familiar forms such as cups, chairs, tables, and bodies in order to topple and reconceive perceptions of "women's work," "home life," and other patriarchal social constructs.

CAMH is a place where art and artists drive conversations about contemporary life. One of the institution's most important roles is to be a platform for artists to directly share their work with diverse audiences and thereby impact broader dialogues. Our endeavors range from exhibitions and artist-driven events to ongoing programming for families and youth, which often grant young audiences their first exposure to contemporary art. Our core hope is that by making the sometimes challenging and unexpected ideas of contemporary art accessible to anyone, we will open up new ways of thinking and being in the world. In pursuit of this vision, Contemporary Arts Museum Houston is always free and open to all.

CAMH is extremely grateful to our supporters, who have made this exhibition, catalogue, and related public programming possible. Our presenting sponsor for this exhibition is Agnes Gund, whose cultural leadership and support for artists are renowned and continue to set benchmarks for our field. Additional and crucial support for the exhibition is provided by Leah Bennett, Gladstone Gallery, the Murray-Holman Family Trust, and Pace Gallery. Bridget Donahue, Carol LeWitt, and Cody Fitzsimmons and Christopher Scott have also provided valuable support and funding. We wish to thank The Brown Foundation for its ongoing support of CAMH exhibitions and programs. Sissy and Denny Kempner imparted invaluable leadership in cultivating resources for this exhibition.

We are also grateful to our tour partner, Carnegie Museum of Art, Pittsburgh, in particular Eric Crosby, Henry J. Heinz II Director; and Clarissa Morales, director of collections and exhibition management.

CAMH's exhibitions, catalogues, and public programs are truly a team effort, and this project has been realized collaboratively by our extraordinary staff: Sanjuana Banda, Tim Barkley, Adrianna Benavides, Quincy Berry, Janice Bond, Felice Cleveland, Laura Dickey, Kenya Evans, Monica Hoffman, Bridget Hovell, Hannah Lange, Kristin Massa, Rebecca Matalon, Cheryl Newcomb, Beth Peré, Sue Pruden, Mike Reed, Patricia Restrepo, Jeff Shore, Seba Suber, Kent Michael Smith, and YET Torres.

All of CAMH's programs and exhibitions are made possible through the leadership, vision, and support of our trustees, who each bring passion and specific expertise to their roles as stewards of this institution.

Most importantly, I want to offer deep thanks to Jessi Reaves, the Estate of Elizabeth Murray, and the museum's audience. CAMH exists to bring together artists and audience. It is the reciprocal relationship—rooted in discovery and friction—that makes our work come to life. Thank you for your engagement with this exhibition and for your enduring belief in Contemporary Arts Museum Houston.

Hesse McGraw
Executive Director, Contemporary Arts Museum Houston

CURATOR'S ACKNOWLEDGMENTS

Organizing an exhibition of this scale and complexity is no small matter. It is born from the labor, insight, and enthusiasm of all my colleagues at Contemporary Arts Museum Houston, and I thank each and every one of them for their contributions to the realization of Wild Life: Elizabeth Murray & Jessi Reaves.

I must first thank Hesse McGraw, executive director, for his support and enthusiasm for this project. I am also enormously grateful to former deputy director Christina Brungardt, who green-lit Wild Life and who was an early and eager champion of the show. Current deputy director Janice Bond gracefully picked up the reins with aplomb and compassion. In addition, CAMH's exhibitions team has skillfully worked to realize a logistically complex project with the utmost care and consideration, and I extend my sincere appreciation to all of them: Tim Barkley, registrar; Kenya Evans, gallery supervisor; Iva Kinnaird, preparator; Jeff Shore, head preparator; and Amy Strickland, assistant registrar. For her efforts in fundraising for this exhibition, I thank Cheryl Newcomb, director of development. I reserve my most heartfelt thanks for Patricia Restrepo, exhibitions manager and assistant curator, without whose attention to detail and unparalleled work ethic this exhibition would not have been possible.

The development of this publication is the result of the dedication and rigor of our copublishers Karen Kelly and Barbara Schroeder of Dancing Foxes Press. I am immensely honored to have had their oversight and keen editorial eye on this project. The book's design was thoughtfully conceived by Eric Wrenn, whose commitment to creating a space to honor both Elizabeth Murray and Jessi Reaves is reflected in the pages of this publication. From the outset, the catalogue was subject to the challenges inherent in bringing together the individual voices of two artists, one of whom is no longer with us. Rather than disregard these challenges, amplified by the issue of time and the generations that separate Murray and Reaves, Eric used them to shape the design. A landmark interview between Kate Horsfield and Elizabeth Murray, originally published in a 1986 issue of Profile magazine, runs throughout. The direction, format, and design of this interview are mirrored in a newly commissioned conversation between Johanna Fateman and Jessi Reaves, which further bridges past and present. I am grateful to Fateman, Reaves, and Horsfield for playing along, and to Video Data Bank for permitting us to reprint the 1986 interview. I am also thankful for the work of my colleague Kent Michael Smith, director of communications and marketing, who has newly taken on the role of overseeing all of CAMH's publications. Kristin Massa, videographer, produced the beautiful panoramic installation view included in this catalogue and Sean Fleming the focused views, and I am grateful for their vision.

I wish to extend my sincere gratitude to the following individuals who have generously offered key insights and feedback on Wild Life: Connie Butler, Paula Cooper, Dean Daderko, Kate Horsfield, Fredericka Hunter, Anna Katz, Adam Marnie, Amy Sillman, and Robert Storr. Many artists, curators, dealers, administrators, and collectors contributed significant time and energy to assist in my research, at times opening their institutions and homes to me. I thank you all: Ann Goldstein and Jay Dandy at the Art Institute of Chicago; Bridget Donahue, Erin Leland, and Sabrina Tamar at Bridget Donahue, New York; Julie Aronson at the Cincinnati Art Museum; Emily Liebert at the Cleveland Museum of Art; Adrienne Atkins at the Marguerite Hoffman Collection; Michelle White at the Menil Collection, Houston; Rachel Federman at the Morgan Library and Museum, New York; Alison de Lima Green at Museum of Fine Arts, Houston; Lilian Tone at the Museum of Modern Art, New York; Tiffany Raulerson at the Orlando Museum of Art, Florida; Douglas Baxter and Alexander Brown at Pace Gallery, New York; Zachary Vanes at Video Data Bank, Chicago; Jennie Goldstein and Lawrence Hernandez at Whitney Museum of American Art, New York; Kaleta Doolin and Alan Govenar; Sam and Erin Falls; Heidi and David Gerger; Helen Hill and Denny Kempner; Bob Holman; Daisy Murray Holman and Michael Walker; Mr. and Mrs. Marvin Rappaport; Elizabeth Smith; and Julia Trotta.

This exhibition would not have been possible without the support of Jason Andrew of the Estate of Elizabeth Murray. His commitment to providing access, information, and guidance, as well as his willingness to share his wealth of knowledge on Murray's work have been exceptional. In this measure, I wish to thank all of the members of the Murray-Holman Family Trust who have generously let me into their homes and recounted their memories, permitted me access to Murray's journals, and been tremendous supporters of this project from beginning to end. Thank you to Elizabeth Murray's husband, Bob Holman, and to her three children, Dakota Sunseri, Sophie Ellsberg, and Daisy Murray Holman.

Finally, I extend my utmost gratitude to the artists: Elizabeth Murray and Jessi Reaves. While my access to Murray has been through her works, writing, and reception, it has been an honor to dig deeply into and intimately appreciate four decades of her art making, even in her absence. It has been a pure joy to work with Reaves, who has committed herself fully to this exhibition. She has been an exceptional partner over the past two years, and I have learned much from both her work and the insights she has offered, as an artist, on Murray's paintings. It is not always the case that a collaboration of this kind leads to friendship, but I am thankful that it has. Most significantly, I am grateful for everything Murray and Reaves have shown me about the pleasures of falling apart.

I dedicate this catalogue to C. R. W.

Rebecca Matalon
Curator, Contemporary Arts Museum Houston

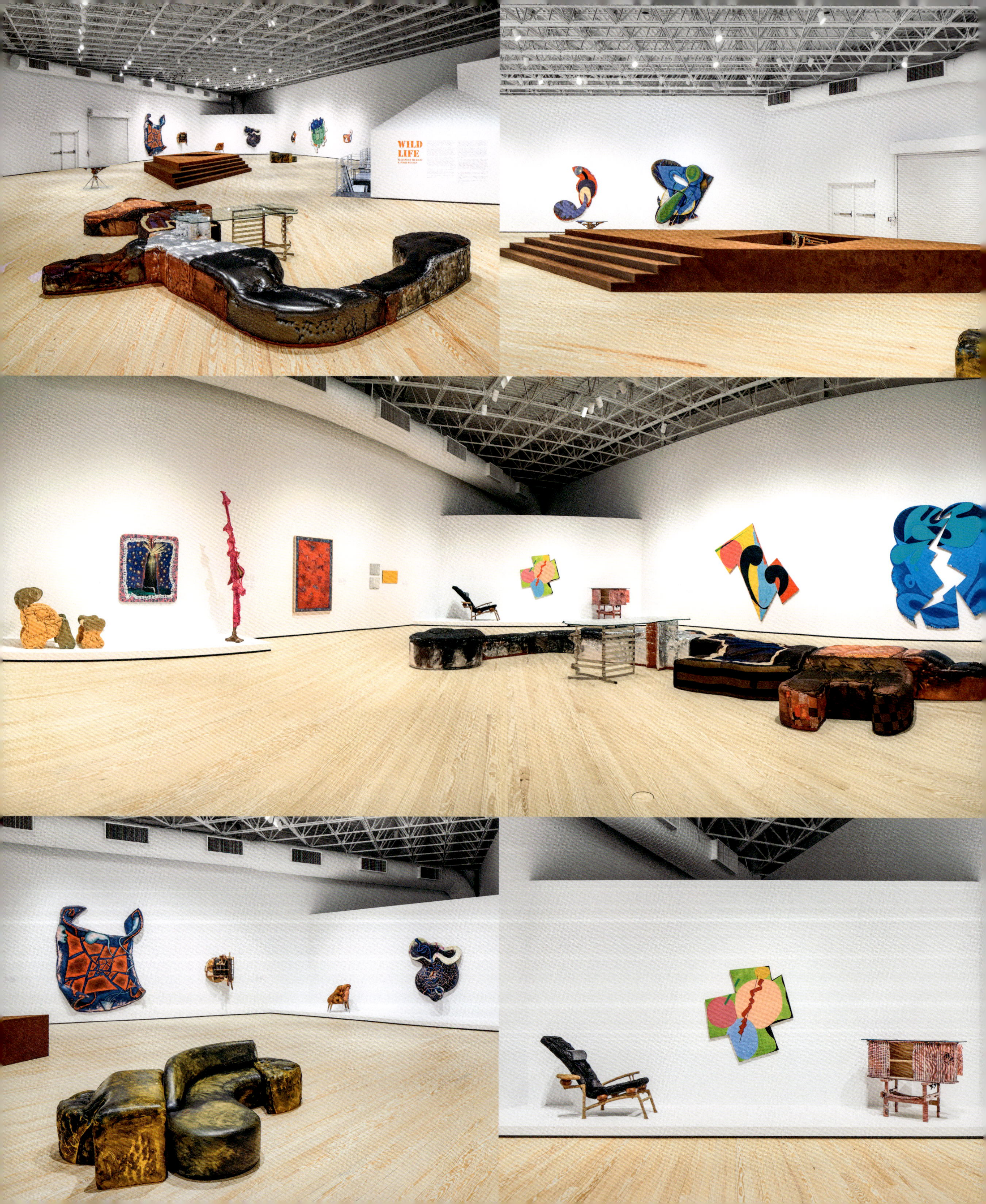
WILD
LIFE

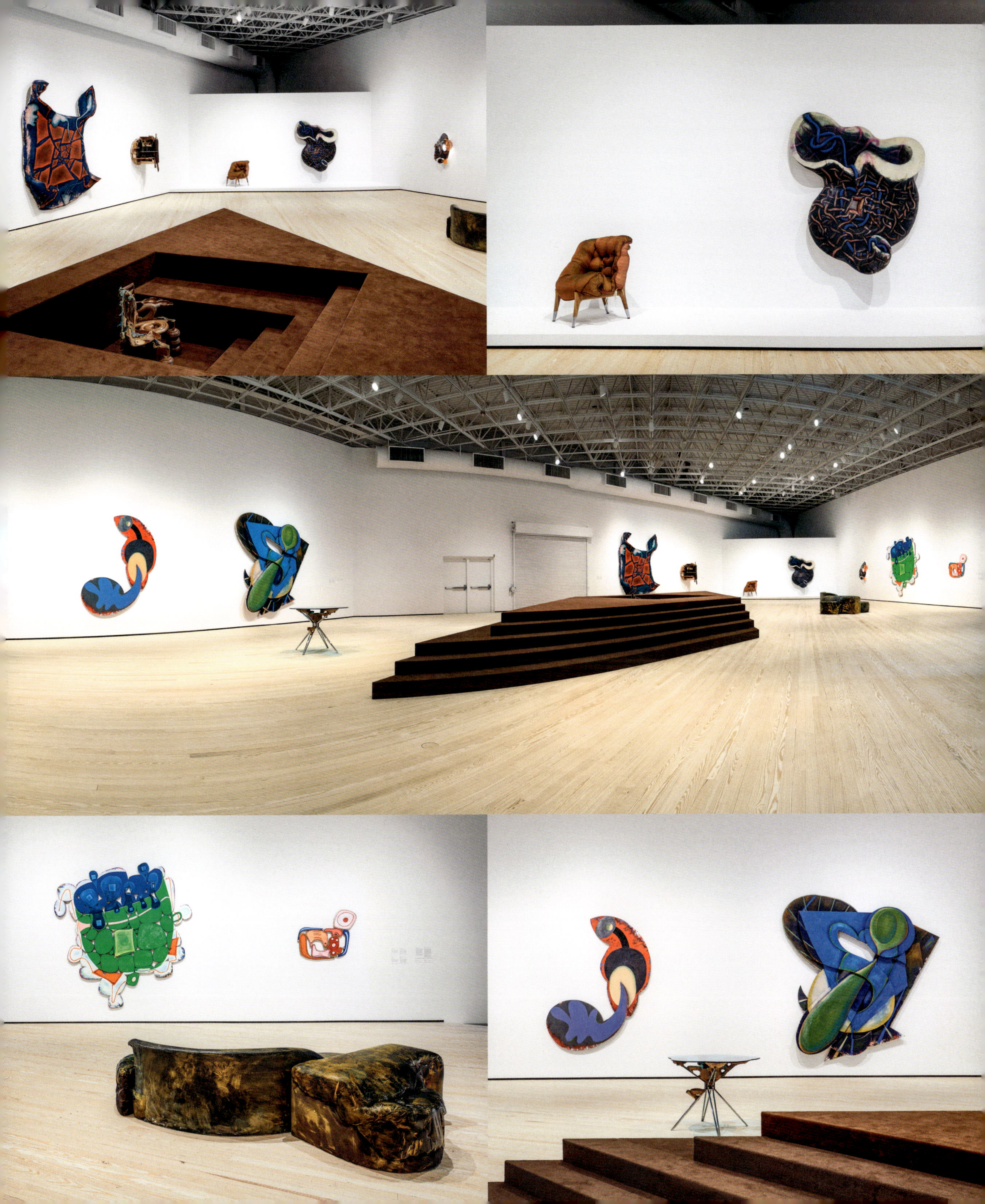

Elizabeth Murray (b. 1940, Chicago; d. 2007, New York) earned a BFA from the School of the Art Institute of Chicago in 1962 and an MFA from Mills College, Oakland, California, in 1964. In 1967, she moved to New York City. Murray's work has been the subject of nearly sixty solo exhibitions in galleries around the world since her New York debut in the 1972 Annual Exhibition at the Whitney Museum of American Art, New York. It has been featured in six Whitney Biennials since. A comprehensive exhibition including more than seventy-five paintings and works on paper was presented at the Museum of Modern Art, New York, in 2005. Murray received numerous awards, including the Skowhegan Medal for Painting in 1986 and a MacArthur Foundation "genius" award in 1999. In addition to her teaching position at Bard College, Annandale-on-Hudson, New York, Murray held visiting faculty appointments at a number of American colleges and universities throughout her life.

Jessi Reaves (b. 1986, Portland, Oregon) earned her BFA from Rhode Island School of Design, Providence, in 2009. Reaves's solo exhibitions include *Going Out in Style*, Herald St, London (2019); *Jessi Reaves II*, Bridget Donahue, New York (2019); *Kitchen Arrangement*, a site-specific commission for *The Domestic Plane: New Perspectives on Tabletop Art Objects*, the Aldrich Contemporary Art Museum, Ridgefield, Connecticut (2018); *android stroll*, Herald St, London (2017); *Jessi Reaves*, Bridget Donahue, New York (2016); and *Now Showing: Jessi Reaves*, SculptureCenter, Long Island City, New York (2016). Recent group exhibitions include *Slant Step Forward*, Verge Center for the Arts, Sacramento, California (2019); Carnegie International, 57th Edition, Carnegie Museum of Art, Pittsburgh (2018); *Ginny Casey and Jessi Reaves*, Institute of Contemporary Art, Philadelphia (2017); Whitney Biennial, Whitney Museum of American Art, New York (2017); and *Looking Back*, the eleventh White Columns Annual, White Columns, New York (2017), among others.

Johanna Fateman is a writer, art critic, and musician, and an owner of Seagull Salon in New York. She was a member of the band Le Tigre beginning in 1999, and in 2009 donated her papers to the Riot Grrrl Collection at New York University's Fales Library and Special Collections. She now regularly writes art reviews for the *New Yorker* and is a contributing editor of *Artforum*; she has also written for *Aperture*, *Art in America*, *Bookforum*, and the *New York Review of Books*. She is coeditor of *Last Days at Hot Slit: The Radical Feminism of Andrea Dworkin*, published by Semiotext(e) in 2019, and is currently at work on a novel.

Kate Horsfield is an American artist, author, and educator who has focused her work on video art and video documentation. In 1976, with Lyn Blumenthal she cofounded Video Data Bank, an international video-art distribution organization. Together Horsfield and Blumenthal also produced more than ninety in-depth video interviews with visual and performance artists, critics, and photographers such as Romare Bearden, Joseph Beuys, Buckminster Fuller, Lee Krasner, Agnes Martin, and Marcia Tucker, from 1974 to 1988. As an educator, Horsfield periodically taught courses at the School of the Art Institute of Chicago, the University of Illinois at Chicago, and the University of Texas at Austin. After the death of Blumenthal in 1988, Horsfield was executive director of Video Data Bank until 2006. She currently lives and works in New York.

Rebecca Matalon is curator at Contemporary Arts Museum Houston (CAMH), where she recently organized *Garrett Bradley: American Rhapsody* (2019), the first solo museum presentation of the work of artist and filmmaker Garrett Bradley. Previously, Matalon was assistant curator at the Museum of Contemporary Art, Los Angeles (MoCA), where she organized exhibitions including *Tongues Untied* (2015), *Mickalene Thomas: Do I Look Like a Lady?* (2016), *Welcome to the Dollhouse* (2018), and *Décor: Barbara Bloom, Andrea Fraser, Louise Lawler* (2018). In 2018, she co-organized *Zoe Leonard: Survey*, a major midcareer retrospective of the work of Zoe Leonard. Matalon is cofounder and, from 2015 to 2019, curator of JOAN, a not-for-profit exhibition space in Los Angeles that is dedicated to presenting the work of emerging and underrepresented artists. She serves on the board of Electronic Arts Intermix (EAI) and is on the Organizing Committee of Texas Talks Art, a multi-institutional initiative that launched in January 2021.

Lenders to the Exhibition

Hope Atherton and Gavin Brown, New York
Eleanor and Bobby Cayre, New York
Bridget Donahue, New York
John and Lisa Dorn, Houston
Sam and Erin Falls, Los Angeles
Dr. Robert Feldman, Cohoes, New York
Heidi and David Gerger, Houston
Gladstone Gallery, New York and Brussels
Marguerite Steed Hoffman
Helen Hill Kempner, Houston
Clare Casademont and Michael Metz, Houston
The Murray-Holman Family Trust, New York
Arthur and Susan Murray Resnick, Hollywood, Florida
The Museum of Fine Arts, Houston
Paul Pincus, New York
Carolyn Ramo, New York
Dr. and Mrs. Marvin Rappaport
Ellen Phelan and Joel Shapiro, New York

CAMH Staff

Hesse McGraw, Executive Director
Sanjuana Banda, Graphic Designer
Tim Barkley, Registrar
Adrianna Benavides, Teen Council and Tour Programs Coordinator
Quincy Berry, Assistant Gallery Supervisor
Janice Bond, Deputy Director
Felice Cleveland, Director of Education and Public Programs
Laura Dickey, Grants Coordinator
Kenya Evans, Gallery Supervisor
Monica Hoffman, Controller
Bridget Hovell, Membership Coordinator
Hannah Lange, Communications Coordinator
Kristin Massa, Videographer
Rebecca Matalon, Curator
Cheryl Newcomb, Director of Development
Beth Peré, Senior Events Manager
Sue Pruden, Director of Retail Operations
Mike Reed, Assistant Director of Facilities and Risk Management
Patricia Restrepo, Exhibitions Manager and Assistant Curator
Jeff Shore, Head Preparator
Kent Michael Smith, Director of Communications and Marketing
Seba Suber, Director of Finance and Strategic Initiatives
YET Torres, Public Programs Coordinator

Exhibition Donors and Patrons

Nora and Bob Ackerley
Chinhui and Eddie Allen
The Brown Foundation, Inc., of Houston
George and Mary Josephine Hamman Foundation
Blakely and Trey Griggs
Houston Endowment, Inc.
John R. Eckel Jr. Foundation
Sissy and Denny Kempner
Lucinda and Javier Loya
M. D. Anderson Foundation
National Endowment for the Arts
Rea Charitable Trust
River Oaks District
The Sarofim Foundation
Louisa Stude Sarofim
Texas Commission on the Arts
Phoebe Tudor
Wallace S. Wilson
Marion and David Young

Presenting sponsorship for *Wild Life: Elizabeth Murray & Jessi Reaves* has been provided by Agnes Gund with additional support from Leah Bennett, Gladstone Gallery, The Murray-Holman Family Trust, and Pace Gallery. Additional funding provided by Carol LeWitt and Cody Fitzsimmons and Christopher Scott.

Publication support provided by Bridget Donahue, New York.

Contemporary Arts Museum Houston is funded in part by the City of Houston through Houston Arts Alliance.

Artist Benefactors

Andisheh Avini
Rhona Bitner
Will Boone
Robert Bordo
Billy Childish
Holly Coulis
Cheryl Donegan
Thomas Glassford
Joseph Havel
Jenny Holzer
Paul Kremer
Georgia Marsh
Floyd Newsum
Angel Otero
Aaron Parazette
Eduardo Portillo
Ed Ruscha
Margo Sawyer
Bret Shirley
Peter Sullivan
Nari Ward
Guy Yanai

This book was published on the occasion of the exhibition *Wild Life: Elizabeth Murray & Jessi Reaves*, curated by Rebecca Matalon, curator, Contemporary Arts Museum Houston.

Contemporary Arts Museum Houston, February 24–May 16, 2021

Carnegie Museum of Art, September 3, 2021–January 9, 2022

Edited by Karen Kelly, Rebecca Matalon, and Barbara Schroeder
Editorial assistant: Natalie Colarossi
Proofreading: Polly Watson
Design by Eric Wrenn Office, New York

This book is typeset in Stencil, American Typewriter, Linotype Helvetica Neue, and Schreibmaschine, and printed on Salamander Braun, Perigord Matt, and Enviro Value C.

Printed and bound by Cantz, Riederich, Germany

Published in 2021 by Contemporary Arts Museum Houston and Dancing Foxes Press, Brooklyn, New York

Library of Congress Cataloging-in-Publication Data

Names: Schröder, Barbara, 1969– editor. | Kelly, Karen J., 1964– editor. | Fateman, Johanna, 1974– interviewer. | Matalon, Rebecca. Rude awakening. | Horsfield, Kate. Profile. | Murray, Elizabeth, 1940–2007. Works. Selections. | Reaves, Jessi, 1986– Works. Selections. | Contemporary Arts Museum Houston, organizer, host institution.
Title: Wild life : Elizabeth Murray & Jessi Reaves.
Other titles: Wild life (Contemporary Arts Museum Houston)
Description: Houston : Contemporary Arts Museum ; [Brooklyn] : Dancing Foxes Press, [2021] | Includes bibliographical references. | Summary: "This volume brings together the paintings of Elizabeth Murray (1940-2007) and the work of New York-based sculptor Jessi Reaves (born 1986). Despite the generations that separate Murray and Reaves, this publication highlights each artist's lyrical, playful and rigorous engagements with the decorative, domestic, and bodily"—Provided by publisher.
Identifiers: LCCN 2020058200 | ISBN 9781733688932 (paperback)
Subjects: LCSH: Murray, Elizabeth, 1940–2007—Exhibitions. | Reaves, Jessi, 1986—Exhibitions.
Classification: LCC N6537.M87 A4 2021 | DDC 709.2/2--dc23
LC record available at https://lccn.loc.gov/2020058200

ISBN: 978-1-7336889-3-2

Contemporary Arts Museum Houston
5216 Montrose Boulevard
Houston, TX 77006
camh.org

Dancing Foxes Press
16 Lefferts Place
Brooklyn, NY 11238
dfpress.us

Available through
ARTBOOK | D.A.P.
75 Broad Street, Suite 630
New York, NY 10004
www.artbook.com

Printed in Germany

Photo and Collection Credits:

pp. 16–17 and insert p. 10 top: Collection Ellen Phelan and Joel Shapiro, New York; courtesy Pace Gallery, photo by Kerry Ryan McFate; p. 18: Collection Martin and Rebecca Eisenberg; p. 19: Collection The Murray-Holman Family Trust, New York; p. 20: Collection Arthur and Susan Murray, Resnick, Hollywood, Florida; p. 21: Napoleone Collection, London; pp. 22 and 23: Collection Dennis Freedman; p. 24: Collection Dr. and Mrs. Marvin Rappaport; p. 25: Collection The Murray-Holman Family Trust, New York, courtesy Pace Gallery, photo by G.R. Christmas; pp. 26 (both images) and 27: Private Collection and Herald St, London; p. 28: Collection Pérez Art Museum Miami, museum purchase with funds provided by PAMM's Collectors Council and gift of Pace Gallery, New York, 2019.184; p. 29: Private Collection, courtesy Pace Gallery; p. 30: Collection Heidi and David Gerger, Houston, courtesy Pace Gallery, photo by G.R. Christmas; p. 31: Collection Sue and Al Ravitz; pp. 32–33: Private Collection; p. 34: Collection John and Lisa Dorn, Houston, courtesy Pace Gallery, photo by Ellen Page Wilson; p. 35: A&S Abu Ghazaleh Collection; p. 36: courtesy Pace Gallery, New York; p. 37: Collection Eleanor and Bobby Cayre, New York, courtesy Paula Cooper Gallery, New York, photo by Steven Probert; p. 38: The Museum of Contemporary Art, Los Angeles, The Barry Lowen Collection (85.74A-B); p. 39: Collection The Murray-Holman Family Trust, New York; p. 40: Cincinnati Art Museum, Gift of Douglas S. Cramer, 2006.108, photo by Rob Deslongchamps; p. 41: Collection Hope Atherton and Gavin Brown, New York; p. 48 (top): Private Collection, Monaco; pp. 48–49 (bottom): Private Collection; pp. 50 and 51: Private Collection, Pittsburgh, Pennsylvania; p. 52: The Museum of Fine Arts, Houston, Bequest of Edward R. Broida, 2007.624; p. 53: Collection Dennis Freedman; p. 54: Courtesy The Murray-Holman Family Trust and Gladstone Gallery, New York and Brussels; p. 55: Mima and César Reyes, San Juan; pp. 56–57: Collection Sam and Erin Falls, Los Angeles, California; p. 58: Cleveland Museum of Art, Promised Gift of Agnes Gund in honor of Bob Holman 289.1993; p. 59: Collection Dennis Freedman; p. 60: Private Collection, New York, courtesy Pace Gallery, photo by Ellen Page Wilson; pp. 61 and 63: Private Collection; p. 62: Private Collection, courtesy Pace Gallery, photo by Ellen Page Wilson; pp. 64 and 65: Collection Dennis Freedman; p. 66: Collection Helen Hill Kempner, Houston, courtesy Pace Gallery, photo by Ellen Page Wilson; p. 67: Collection Gabe Schulman, New York; pp. 68–69: Collection Miller Meigs; p. 70: Collection Dr. Robert Feldman, Cohoes, New York, courtesy Paula Cooper Gallery, New York; p. 71: Courtesy Jim Abrams and Mario Russo, San Francisco, and Herald St, London; p. 72: Collection Carnegie Museum of Art, The Henry L. Hillman Fund, 2019.55.2; p. 73: Collection Clare Casademont and Michael Metz, Houston, courtesy Pace Gallery, photo by Ellen Page Wilson; pp. 76–77 (center): photo by Kristin Massa; pp. 76–77 (top row, bottom row): photos by Sean Fleming. Insert cover and p. 2: courtesy of the Video Data Bank at the School of the Art Institute of Chicago, vdb.org; insert p. 10 bottom: courtesy Paula Cooper Gallery, New York

Profile 5, no. 3, "Elizabeth Murray," is reprinted, appropriating the design and layout of the original, by permission of the Video Data Bank (VDB) and Kate Horsfield. The interview originates from Lyn Blumenthal and Horsfield's video *Elizabeth Murray 1977: An Interview*. Between 1974 and 1988, Blumenthal and Horsfield performed ninety video interviews, which serve as the basis for VDB's On Art and Artists collection. Blumenthal and Horsfield founded VDB in 1976 at the School of the Art Institute of Chicago; including the work of over six hundred artists and six thousand video art titles, it has become a leading resource in the United States for video by and about contemporary artists.